BEST PRACTICES IN URBAN SOLID WASTE MANAGEMENT

BEST PRACTICES IN URBAN SOLID WASTE MANAGEMENT

Ownership, Governance, and Drivers of Performance in a Zero Waste Framework

GIULIA ROMANO
University of Pisa, Italy

CLAUDIO MARCIANO
University of Turin, Italy

And

MARIA SILVIA FIORELLI
University of Pisa, Italy

emerald PUBLISHING

United Kingdom – North America – Japan – India
Malaysia – China

Emerald Publishing Limited
Howard House, Wagon Lane, Bingley BD16 1WA, UK

First edition 2021

Reprints and permissions service
Contact: permissions@emeraldinsight.com

British Library Cataloguing in Publication Data
A catalogue record for this book is available from the British Library

ISBN: 978-1-80043-889-7 (Print)
ISBN: 978-1-80043-888-0 (Online)
ISBN: 978-1-80043-890-3 (Epub)

Printed and bound by CPI Group (UK) Ltd, Croydon, CR0 4YY

ISOQAR
REGISTERED
ISOQAR certified Management System, awarded to Emerald for adherence to Environmental standard ISO 14001:2004.
Certificate Number 1985
ISO 14001

INVESTOR IN PEOPLE

CONTENTS

LIST OF TABLES AND FIGURES

LIST OF ABBREVIATIONS

ATO	Optimal Territorial Areas
BSR	Berliner Stadtreinigungsbetriebe
CEO	Chief Executive Officer
DGERT	General Direction of Employment and Labor Relations
EBITDA	Earnings Before Interest, Taxes, Depreciation, and Amortization
EU	European Union
FRZ	Formia Rifiuti Zero
GDP	Gross Domestic Product
HSY	Helsinki Region Environmental Services Authority
KPI	Key Performance Indicators
MOE	Municipally Owned Enterprise
MSW	Municipal Solid Waste
NIMBY	Not In My Backyard
OECD	Organisation for Economic Co-operation and Development
PAP	Personal Absorbent Products
PAYT	Pay As You Throw
PSO	Public Sector Organization
RFID	Radio-Frequency Identification
SDG	Sustainable Development Goal
SGEIs	Services of General Economic Interest
SGIs	Services of General Interest
SOE	State-Owned Enterprise
TBL	Triple Bottom Line
TMW	Take–Make–Waste
WEEE	Waste of Electrical and Electronic Equipment
ZW	Zero Waste
ZWE	Zero Waste Europe
ZWIA	Zero Waste International Alliance

ABOUT THE CONTRIBUTORS

Maria Silvia Fiorelli is Researcher and Teacher of Business Organization at the University of Pisa; She has a Phd in Business Economics. She is authors of papers and books about network and human resources. She teaches Business Organization in Master classes at the University of Pisa.

Latest publications: Fiorelli, M. S. (2019), Family business and leadership models; in *International Journal of Business and Social Science*; Fiorelli, M. S. (2018), Il processo generazionale nelle PMI (analisi e modelli di sviluppo imprenditoriale), ed. Arnus, 988865284414

Claudio Marciano is a Postdoctoral Researcher at University of Turin in Sociology of Economy and Adjunct Professor in Sociology and Politics for Innovation at University of Aosta Valley. His research interests concern sociology of territory with a focus on the urban public policy, local public services, and social innovation. Engaged in several multidisciplinary team of research for private companies and no profit organizations, he was deputy major on charge of urban sustainability and smart cities in Formia Municipality (40.000 inhab.).

Latest publications: Torres, A., Bejarano, J. F., Manzanera, R., Pellizzoni, L., Marciano, C. (2020), A critical analysis of circular economy among Southern Europe: an innovative proposal for environmental degradation and sustainability of life. In "Social Problems in Southern Europe: A Comparative Assessment" (eds Entran Duran, F., Soriano Miras, R. M., Duque Clavache, R.). Southern European Societies, Edward Elgar Publishing, London, ISBN: 978-1-78990-142-9; Marciano, C., Cassone Idone, V., Onnis, E., Paini, G., (2020), Università e Territorio: il modello del Knowledge Interchange. Il caso Piemonte 2029. In Autonomie Locali e Servizi Sociali, n.1/2020, Il Mulino: Bologna. ISSN: 0382-2278

Giulia Romano is Associate Professor of Business Administration, Corporate Governance, and Economics of Public Services. She has the National Scientific Habilitation to Full Professor. She was Scientific Coordinator of the Jean Monnet Module "European Water Utility Management" funded by the EACEA (EU) (2014–2017). She coordinated and participated in many research projects and is author of more than 50 international research articles, books, and book chapters on utility management, waste management, performance analysis, and corporate governance.

Latest publications: Minoja, M., Romano, G. (2021), Managing intellectual capital for sustainability: Evidence from a Re-municipalized, publicly owned waste management firm, *Journal of Cleaner Production*, 279, 123213; Romano, G., Masserini, L., Lombardi, G. V. (2021). Environmental performance of waste management: Impacts of corruption and public maladministration in Italy. *Journal of Cleaner Production*, 288, 125521; Romano, G., Molinos-Senante, M. (2020), Factors affecting eco-efficiency of municipal waste services in Tuscan municipalities: An empirical investigation of different management models, *Waste Management*, 105, 384–394; Romano, G., Rapposelli, A., Marrucci, L. (2019), Improving waste production and recycling through zero waste strategy and privatization: An empirical investigation, *Resources, Conservation & Recycling*, 146, 256–263

ACKNOWLEDGMENTS

Giulia Romano and Maria Silvia Fiorelli acknowledge financial support from the University of Pisa, PRA 2018.

INTRODUCTION AND METHODOLOGY[1]

ABSTRACT

Public service provision in the European Union has received great attention in the last decades. Waste management is among the most important public services and challenges for a sustainable world owing to its impact on the environment, economic development, human health, and equity. Throughout Europe, along with the circular economy, the related zero waste (ZW) framework is also rapidly spreading. This introduction provides information about research questions and methodology used to discuss the most relevant and critical issues for good management of waste service provision under the ZW framework.

Keywords: Public service; waste management; European Union; zero waste framework; best practice; case studies

Public service provision in the European Union (EU) has received great attention in the last decades. Public services such as drinking water provision, urban waste collection and treatment, and transport are essential for granting an adequate quality of life and supporting the unification process, by allowing European citizens to benefit from a standard level of public service quantity and quality. Good public services are regarded as pillars of the European model of well-being and development, as they affect the general interest of communities at the local, regional, and national levels; they can even influence migration policies, owing to their impact on the environment, sanitation, and health. Their relevance requires specific public service obligations as they can be provided either by the public or by the private sector.

Transition toward a circular economy is not only a critical need for global policy but also an opportunity to enhance the relevance of protecting the environment for business success and sustainability. Waste management is among the most important public services and challenges for a sustainable world owing to its impact on the environment, economic development, human health, and equity.

1 This chapter was written by Giulia Romano.

Waste is defined by the Waste Framework Directive (Directive 2008/98/EC) Article 3(1) as *any substance or object which the holder discards or intends or is required to discard.* Currently, urban waste management is under increasing pressure, given the worldwide challenges of population, urban, and gross domestic product (GDP) growth, and the threat of global climate change. Indeed, recent communication from the European Commission is called "A New Circular Economy Action Plan for a Cleaner and More Competitive Europe," and started by saying that

> *...there is only one planet Earth, yet by 2050, the world will be consuming as if there were three. The global consumption of materials such as biomass, fossil fuels, metals, and minerals is expected to double in the next forty years, while annual waste generation is projected to increase by 70% by 2050.*
>
> (European Commission, 2020a)

According to the European Commission, the transition to circular economy principles could support the increase of EU GDP by an additional 0.5% by 2030 and create around 700,000 new jobs (Cambridge Econometrics, Trinomics, and ICF, 2018). Further, European firms could increase their profitability by reducing their costs for materials and better shield their accounts from resource price fluctuations (European Commission, 2020a).

For the waste sector, transitioning toward a circular economy presents an opportunity to promote organizational changes and improve performance from a broad perspective, which encompasses economic, financial, environmental, social, and even accountability issues.

Several challenges currently affect the waste industry. The waste sector is a particularly delicate and complex industry that presents problems affecting several aspects worldwide, from organized crime and corruption to public versus private management conflict, lack of proper plants, and strategic planning.

At the European level, data from the last two decades showed that urban waste generation increased; however, the most recent trend highlights a marked tendency to decrease waste generation, in accordance with the first step of a successful waste policy: waste reduction. Along with waste reduction and reuse, separate waste collection is a relevant step to sustainable waste management and meeting circular economy targets (BiPRO/CRI, 2015). Indeed, it could support effective recycling and composting activities, and realize a real recovery of waste, avoiding the disposal of material and energy losses.

Recently, in 2019, the European Investment Bank decided to refrain from financing the municipal waste incinerator in Belgrade, Serbia, by highlighting that incinerators tend to crowd out waste prevention and recycling measures (CEE Bankwatch Network, 2019). Thus, at the European level, along with waste directive and action plans, financial institutions are also fostering the circular economy by avoiding supporting unsustainable practices that can reduce the efforts to increase recycling and composting.

Considering exemplary cases of waste management firms and municipalities that have implemented effective innovations in the management of urban waste services in well-developed European countries such as Italy is of utmost importance. As a matter of fact, waste management services are not only economic activities but also key environmental and societal issues, needing innovation at managerial and technological levels. Economic, social, and environmental aspects of waste management activities should be considered in the impact assessment of policy options (BIO Intelligence Service, 2011a) as well as in performance assessment using the triple bottom line (TBL) approach (Elkington, 1997, 1998).

Throughout Europe, along with the circular economy, the related zero waste (ZW) framework is also rapidly spreading, owing to innovation in legislation and regulation and to the increasing relevance of citizens' concerns about a more sustainable way of living, waste production, and treatment.

This book aims to discuss the most relevant and critical issues for good management of waste service provision under the ZW framework: ownership and corporate governance, performance measurement based on the TBL approach, key drivers of good waste management (innovation, responsibility, stakeholder engagement through communication and training, and knowledge sharing), and discussing the relationships among these issues.

A selection of case studies of urban waste management operators will be presented throughout the text, ranging from well-developed waste management firms to start-ups created after remunicipalization processes, from firms with complex ownership and governance characteristics to sole shareholder firms, from firms realizing internally developed innovations to firms that have realized joint ventures and collaboration with several partners. Most cases are derived from the Italian waste management experience, which is considered internationally relevant and pioneering in the European ZW framework. Other cases concern European experiences.

Successful best practices in urban waste management realized by cutting-edge firms and municipalities will be used to provide relevant examples, considering their collection methods, tariff setting systems, collaborations, and knowledge sharing processes with partners and providers, recycling procedures, and employees' and stakeholders' engagement programs.

We chose the "multiple case design" (Bourgeois & Eisenhardt, 1988; Eisenhardt & Graebner, 2007), to access to information not available from publicly available sources.

Our research questions were as follows:

(1) Which are the key drivers of sustainable urban solid waste management?

(2) How does ownership affect these key drivers?

(3) How do these drivers affect the performance of urban waste operators?

(4) What is the role of different social actors, such as grassroots movements, local public administrations, and innovative start-ups, to foster key drivers?

A multiple case approach allows treating a series of cases as a series of experiments in replication logic. Each case study can corroborate or disprove the suppositions drawn from the preceding one (Yin, 1984).

These case studies were selected using the snowball sampling technique. After a careful analysis of existing literature and documentation available, we started by interviewing a well-known manager of several Italian waste utilities with relevant experiences in different contexts.

Following this initial interview, we identified four other important professionals in the waste management industry, chosen as key informants about the "zero waste" framework. We, thus, held unstructured interviews with a well-known activist, leader of the "zero waste" movement in Italy and Europe, and the winner of the Goldman Environmental Prize; a technical and EU waste legislation expert and researcher, with decades of experience in separate collection, recycling, composting, and prevention; a manager that directed many relevant waste utilities in Italy; and a former alderman of a well-functioning Italian municipality for waste management activities, who later became the manager of several relevant waste utilities.

Furthermore, a focus group lasting four hours was organized to discuss the experiences of three of the above-mentioned key informants. Then, we identified other key informants to be interviewed, owing to their relevant experiences, and new case studies were identified, owing to their best practice role.

After preliminary contacts, key informants were selected for each case study, that is, officers with substantial or direct responsibilities for strategy definition, communication activities, and innovation process development.

Informal discussions, on-site observations, and document studies were performed along with meetings. Interviews and other documents were processed and interviews transcribed (Corvellec, Bramryd, & Hultman, 2011).

This study adopted an iterative process (Eisenhardt, 1989; Glaser & Strauss, 1967). Divers data collection methods were combined (Eisenhardt, 1989): analysis of archival sources (e.g., annual reports, websites, sustainability reports, informative materials, organization charts, and other provided documentation) and in-depth interviews.

According to the suggestion of López-Gamero, Zaragoza-Sáez, Claver-Cortés, and Molina-Azorín (2011) and as in Minoja and Romano (2021), internal and external validity and reliability tests were carried out with real-time amendments on data to fit emerging knowledge (Eisenhardt, Graebner, & Sonenshein, 2016). Iterations and follow-ups were conducted with the interviewees. Email, telephone calls, and informal meetings were realized to obtain feedback and further information.

Each investigator recorded all the data collected during the interview, taking notes of their impressions (Yin, 1984). After generating preliminary theory with the within-case analysis, we examined similarities and divergence between cases (Eisenhardt, 1989). The comparison among cases allowed us to define whether an emergent outcome was replicated in other cases (Eisenhardt & Graebner, 2007) (Table 1).

Table 1. An Overview of the Urban Waste Management Operator Case Studies.

Waste Operator	Country	Year of Foundation	Ownership	Revenues (2018)	% RD (Last Available Data)
ASCIT SpA	Italy	2004	Public	16,728,476	82.4%
Contarina SpA	Italy	1989	Public	78,559,805	85.6%
Formia Rifiuti Zero SpA	Italy	2014	Public	7,340,274	67.6%
HSY	Finland	2009	Public	99,300,000 (waste management only)	48%
LIPOR	Portugal	1982	Public	39,600,000	41%
Ponte Servizi Srl	Italy	2007	Public	1,209,407 (2017)	90.3%
Voka Snaga	Slovenia	1890	Public	47,090,241	68%

Source: Our elaborations from data available on AIDA and corporate website.

Given the complexity of challenges and expected results of urban waste management in developed countries, a multidisciplinary perspective was assumed, which encompassed management, economic, environmental, and sociological issues.

The book will provide an outlook of reflections on relevant topics and case studies that demonstrate the ability of municipalities and waste utilities to use opportunities for innovating, networking, and knowledge sharing to exploit synergies and value creation processes.

The first chapter of the book provides an overview of the urban waste management sector in Europe, its characteristics, evolution, and perspectives given the normative framework in force and main sustainability challenges, while introducing the circular economy approach and the increasingly relevant ZW strategy.

The second chapter is dedicated to the ZW framework regarding cultural hegemony, genealogy, and social movement, which are derived from sociological theory and are useful for analyzing the phenomenon. Additionally, the reconstruction of the most relevant topics, events, and social actors that spread ZW globally in competition/alternative with the traditional system of waste collection and treatment is provided. Further, it describes the Italian case, one of the geographical contexts where the strategy has been most consolidated and where it is possible to observe more clearly both the knowledge exchange between movements and companies and the connection with the theme of republicization of local public services.

Chapter 3 describes the characteristics and perspectives of the different management models for European urban waste management operators, describing the role of different ownership (public vs. private; direct vs. delegated) in shaping strategies and targets. Further, the remunicipalization process in public service provision is described by considering some existing experiences.

Chapter 4 discusses the importance of the TBL approach in performance measurement for urban waste operators, stressing the need to measure and compare performance, avoiding the pure reference to financial and economic results. Instead, it is of utmost importance to include social and environmental results, in terms of quality of service provided, contribution to environmental sustainability, affordability of tariffs, etc.

Chapter 5 describes the key drivers of good urban waste management, that is, innovation, shared responsibility, stakeholder engagement through communication and training, and knowledge sharing, creating a growing network of knowledge shared among managers, policymakers, civil servants, citizens, and associations. These four drivers mutually reinforce each other and should be developed synergistically by waste managers to define a sustainable waste management system, inspired by existing best practices and that could spread its advantages in benefit of citizens and local governments, beyond the territories served.

Chapter 6 develops a conceptual framework to generalize the empirical evidence and best practices described in the book. A description of the linkages among ownership and management models of waste operators, key management drivers of successful urban waste management, and performance in a TBL approach is provided in the conceptual model, highlighting the relationships among shareholders, business models, and the joint achievement of economic, environmental, and social results.

Special thanks should be devoted to all the managers, policymakers, and researchers who gave us the opportunity to realize interviews and direct visits, that participated in a focus group and a workshop giving us the opportunity to obtain relevant information about relevant best practices in waste management throughout Italy and Europe. Regarding Capannori and its public waste utility Ascit Servizi Ambientali SpA (ASCIT), we interviewed Roger Bizzarri and Maurizio Gatti, actual General Manager and Chairman of ASCIT, the publicly owned waste utility of Capannori, respectively; Alessio Ciacci, the former environment alderman of Capannori, who then became manager of several relevant waste utilities and a start-up for waste management called Minerva; Rossano Ercolini, Goldman Environmental Prize 2013, former president of ASCIT. We interviewed Paolo Contò, the executive director of the Priula Consortium that owns Contarina SpA, a cutting-edge waste utility operating in the Veneto Region, Italy; data gathered through direct interviews for studying the Contarina case were also used (Minoja & Romano, 2021); Enzo Favoino, a technical and EU waste legislation expert and researcher, with decades of experience in separate collection, recycling, composting, and prevention; Raphael Rossi, a manager that directed and administered many relevant waste utilities throughout Italy; Walter Ganapini, scientist, former Italian public manager and alderman, cofounder of Legambiente, and former president of Greenpeace Italia; Nina Sankovič and Vanja Fabjan of Voka Snaga in Ljubljana, Slovenia; Susana Lopes, technician of the International Business Unit, LIPOR, in Greater Porto area in Portugal; Andrea Weckman and Elina Mattero-Meronen, Helsinki Region Environmental Services HSY; Attilio Tornavacca, scientist and founder of ESPER; Roberto Cavallo, founder of ERICA and environmentalist activist.

Our gratitude goes to all the informants we met and interviewed for their support and for sharing with us their experiences and knowledge.

Finally, we gratefully acknowledge the support of the University of Pisa, which financed the Progetti di Ricerca di Ateneo (PRA) 2018 project "Performance and knowledge management of water and waste utilities in the Circular Economy framework," coordinated by Giulia Romano. All the members of the research team and coauthors of papers written during the two-year PRA project period, which were realized with fruitful discussions, deserve special thanks.

1

URBAN WASTE MANAGEMENT IN EUROPE: CHALLENGES AND OPPORTUNITIES[1]

ABSTRACT

This chapter provides an overview of waste management across Europe. It offers an outlook of evolution of waste generation and how European Union (EU) countries treat waste, by providing historical and current data as well as by describing a few best practices of waste management companies and municipalities throughout Europe. The circular economy framework applied to urban waste management and the zero waste strategy are described.

Keywords: Urban waste management; recycling; waste generation; waste treatment; zero waste; circular economy

1.1 URBAN WASTE MANAGEMENT SERVICE IN EUROPE: A BRIEF OVERVIEW OF EVOLUTION AND TREND

Public service provision has been the focus of a relevant debate throughout European Union (EU) policymakers as they are considered substantial pillars of the EU society model. Public services *are those activities which are enshrined within the notion of public good or service based on universality of access for the citizenry rather than the private provision through a market. It is assumed these "public services" should be available for all members of the given society, supplied in an equitable fashion* (Broadbent & Guthrie, 2008).

1 This chapter was written by Giulia Romano.

The term "public service" in the EU framework has been mainly substituted by the term "service of general interest" to avoid ambiguity in its meaning; in fact, it has been highlighted that "public service" is used only in the field of transport but *outside this area, the term is sometimes used in an ambiguous way; it can relate to the fact that a service is offered to the general public and/or in the public interest, or it can be used for the activity of entities in public ownership* (European Commission, 2011). Therefore, EU public service framework focuses on the notion of "services of general interest" (SGIs), that are defined as *services that public authorities of the EU member countries classify as being of general interest and therefore, subject to specific public service obligations. They can be provided either by the state or by the private sector* (European Commission, 2020b) and that could be subdivided into three SGI categories: economic, noneconomic, and social.

This definition highlighted the adoption of an approach that focuses on services instead of providers, so that an SGI is qualified in that way even if it is provided by a private operator.

Ownership is irrelevant for EU policymakers, who do not impose specific criteria for the choice of the SGI provider to Member States, and the same rules should apply equally to public, mixed-owned, and completely private operators.

Thus, the focus is on the services provided, considering their relevance and impact: *SGIs help people lead dignified lives and ensure that everyone has the right to access essential goods and services. They ensure justice, social cohesion and social integration and contribute to the equal treatment of all EU citizens* (European Economic and Social Committee, 2020). Examples of SGIs are public transport, postal services, and healthcare, along with water and energy supply and waste and sewage disposal.

In accordance with principles of subsidiarity and proportionality, the organization, delivery, and financing of SGIs are primarily a competence of Member States to be determined at national, regional, or local levels. As mentioned, some SGIs are Services of General Economic Interest (SGEI), which are *economic activities which deliver outcomes in the overall public good that would not be supplied (or would be supplied under different conditions in terms of quality, safety, affordability, equal treatment or universal access) by the market without public intervention*. Therefore, each Member State has discretion in defining what they regard as SGEI, and this definition could change in accordance with the evolution of the social, geographical, economic, and cultural frameworks.

Indeed, as highlighted by the European Commission (2013), *the scope and organisation of SGEIs vary considerably from one Member State to another, depending on the history and culture of public intervention in each Member State. SGEIs are therefore very diverse and disparities may exist in relation to users' needs and preferences because of different geographical, social and cultural situations. Accordingly, it is essentially the responsibility of the public authorities at national, regional or local level to decide the nature and scope of a service of general interest.*

SGIs are subject to specific public service obligations (PSOs); indeed, *the PSO is imposed on the provider by way of an entrustment and on the basis of a general interest criterion which ensures that the service is provided under conditions allowing it to fulfil its mission.*

Among public services, urban waste management is one of the most impactful for environmental sustainability, local health, and quality of life. Additionally, it frequently requires a broader regional and national perspective to be adequately managed (European Commission (2020b). Urban solid waste collection and treatment is a public service with significant impact on the environment, public health, and the well-being of a local area. To receive the waste collection and treatment service, citizens, firms, and organization are requested to pay tariffs, affecting their expenditure and costs. Thus, the efficiency and sustainability achieved in providing this service is of utmost importance at local and national level (Guerrini, Carvalho, Romano, Cunha Marques, & Leardini, 2017; Romano, Rapposelli, & Marrucci, 2019).

Solid waste production and disposal is strictly linked to urbanization, economic development, and standards of living, along with the environmental strategies adopted. According to the European Environmental Agency (2015), global material use increased almost tenfold since 1900, accelerating from an annual growth of 1.3% in 1900–1949 to 3.6% annually in 2000–2009.

Developing regions are responsible for a growing proportion of resource use at global level. Indeed, while Europe and United States were responsible for 19% and 18% of total resource extraction, respectively, in 1980, by 2009 both had decreased to 10%, whereas Asia's share improved from 41% to 57% over the same period (Krausmann et al., 2009).

According to the World Bank data (World Bank, 2012), Organisation for Economic Co-operation and Development (OECD) countries produce almost half of the world's waste, and by 2050, as many persons will live in urban contexts as the population of the whole world in 2000.

Therefore, policymakers and decision-makers are increasingly invested in determining how to best manage urban waste, reduce its environmental and health impacts, and foster a sustainable management of existing resources, thus avoiding the extraction and subsequent transformation of urban waste into waste to be treated, as far as possible.

Municipal solid waste (MSW) management is one of the most important services provided by a city, and fundamental institutional, financial, social, and environmental problems still currently exist (World Bank, 2012). The cities of the world are expected to generate about 2.2 billion tons of solid waste per year, showing a significant increase from 1.3 billion in 2012. Moreover, waste generation rates will more than double over the next 20 years in lower income countries, with a drastic increase in solid waste management costs (World Bank, 2012).

As the 2030 Agenda for Sustainable Development of the United Nations General Assembly confirms (UN, 2015), a substantial reduction of waste through prevention, reduction, recycling, and reuse is a target to be met globally by 2030 (Goal n. 12.5). Currently, several high-income countries recycle at least a fifth of their MSW, while in low- and middle-income countries, accurate data collection is still challenging (World Bank, 2020).

The enlargement of the EU spanned more than 60 years. From six founding countries in 1952, the Union included 28 countries in 2013, spreading from the Atlantic Ocean to the Asian borders, and from Scandinavia to the Mediterranean coast (Fig. 1.1).

The enlargement process provided several opportunities and challenges for decision- and policymakers, including a strong approach for creating a broad area. Here, the standard of living and accepted standards are quite homogenous, thus providing each Member State and public authorities the opportunity to identify which services should be considered as "public services."

Directive 2008/98/EC on waste as amended by Directive (EU) 2018/851 requested that Member States undertake the necessary measures *to encourage the design of products and components of products to reduce their environmental impact and the generation of waste in the course of the production and subsequent use of products* and achieve the following targets:

a. *by 2020, the preparation for re-use and the recycling of waste materials such as at least paper, metal, plastic and glass from households and possibly from other origins as far as these waste streams are similar to waste from households, shall be increased to a minimum of overall 50 % by weight;*

b. *by 2020, the preparation for re-use, recycling and other material recovery, including backfilling operations using waste to substitute other materials, of non-hazardous construction and demolition waste ... shall be increased to a minimum of 70 % by weight;*

c. *by 2025, the preparation for re-use and the recycling of municipal waste shall be increased to a minimum of 55 % by weight;*

d. *by 2030, the preparation for re-use and the recycling of municipal waste shall be increased to a minimum of 60 % by weight;*

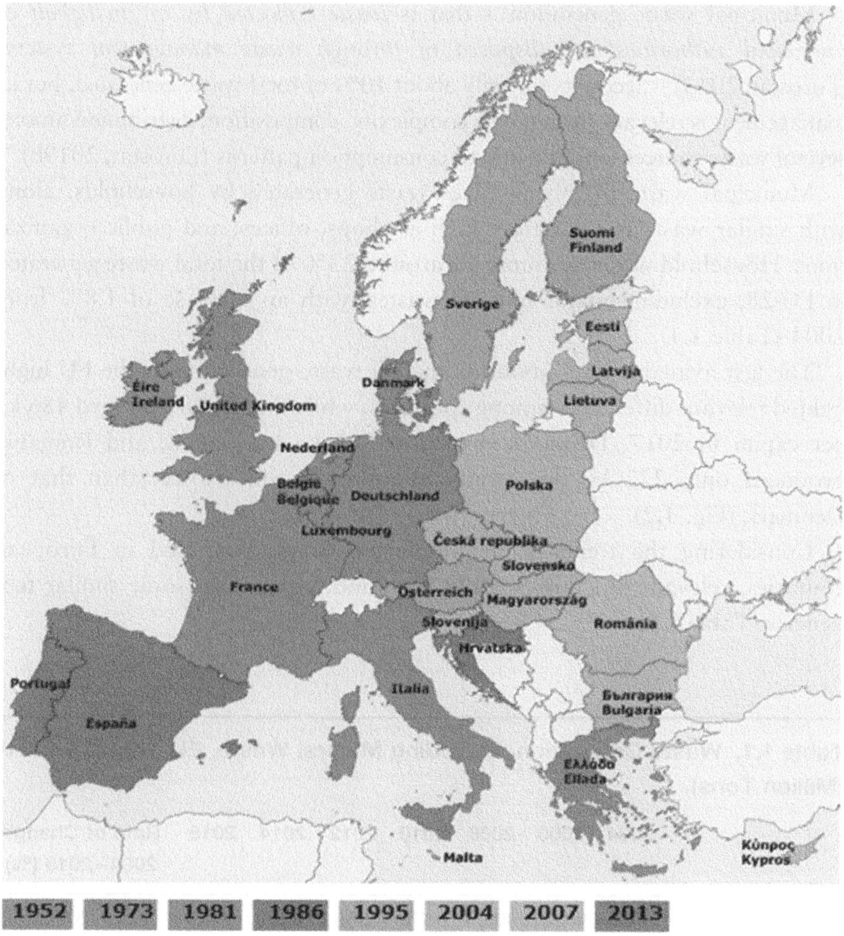

Source: https://europa.eu/european-union/sites/europaeu/files/docs/body/enlargement_it.png

Fig. 1.1. Enlargement Process of the European Union.

e. *by 2035, the preparation for re-use and the recycling of municipal waste shall be increased to a minimum of 65 % by weight (European Commission, 2008).*

Further, Directive 2018/850/EC amending Directive 1999/31/EC sets a target for landfilling:

a. *Member States shall take the necessary measures to ensure that by 2035 the amount of municipal waste landfilled is reduced to 10 % or less of the total amount of municipal waste generated (by weight) (European Commission, 2018).*

Municipal waste generation – that is *waste collected by or on behalf of municipal authorities and disposed of through waste management systems* (Eurostat, 2013) – accounts for only about 10% of total waste generated, but its management is relevant owing to its complexity, composition, distribution among several waste sources, and the link to consumption patterns (Eurostat, 2019b).

Municipal waste mainly involves waste generated by households, along with similar waste from sources such as shops, offices, and public organizations. Household waste accounts for around 23% of the total waste generated in EU-28, excluding major mineral wastes, with an increase of 1.8% from 2004 (Table 1.1).

The last available data about municipal waste generation in the EU highlighted relevant differences among countries, while the EU-28 averaged 486 kg per capita in 2017, Denmark produced 781 kg per capita, and Romania produced only 272 kg per capita, about three times lower than that of Denmark (Fig. 1.2).

Considering the trend of the municipal waste generated in European countries, relevant differences could be found, along with some similar tendencies (Table 1.2).

Table 1.1. Waste Generation, Excluding Mineral Waste, EU-28, 2004–2016 (Million Tons).

	2004	2006	2008	2010	2012	2014	2016	Rate of Change 2004–2016 (%)
Total	940	942.3	903.4	863.1	866	880.3	904.9	−3.7
Agriculture, forestry, and fishing	63.1	57.4	46.2	20.7	21	18.3	20.5	−67.6
Mining and quarrying	10.4	7.1	10.1	7.9	7.8	7.9	7.2	−31.4
Manufacturing	271.4	250.5	236.6	200.9	187.5	185.9	191.2	−29.6
Energy	92.2	100	88.8	81.6	93.4	90.1	76.1	−17.4
Waste/water	110.9	110.2	130.1	144.8	177.5	209.2	228	105.7
Construction	39.3	45.2	38.7	46	42.9	41.9	40.9	3.9
Other sectors	147.7	160.9	140.6	146.8	128.5	124.4	132.3	−10.4
Households	205	211	212.3	214.4	207.4	202.7	208.7	1.8

Source: Our elaboration on Eurostat data.

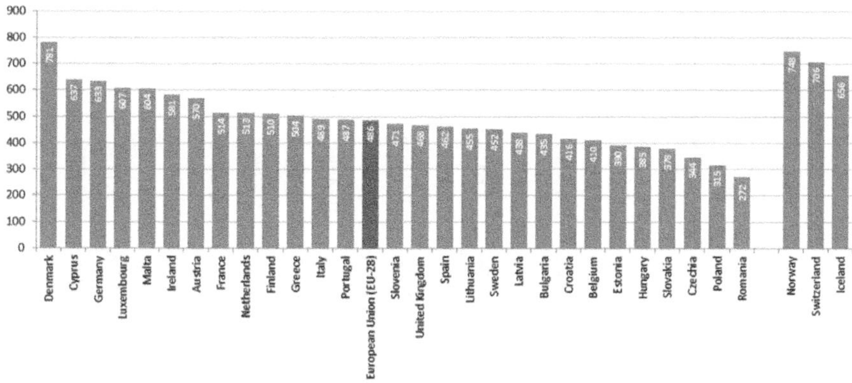

Source: Eurostat, https://ec.europa.eu/eurostat/documents/4187653/10004162/municipal+waste+generated

Fig. 1.2. Municipal Waste Generated (kg per Capita) in 2017.

First, it should be noted that in the last decade (2007–2017), the great majority of European countries experienced a decrease in waste generation per capita, with the EU-28 average reporting a decrease >7%. However, extending the investigated period to the whole available time span (1995–2017), the trend still showed a prevalence of countries showing an increase in waste generation per capita, with an average of 3.4% increase at EU-28 level.

Countries with the highest increase range from the north of the Union (Latvia and Denmark) to the south (Malta and Greece). Significantly, all the founding countries (Belgium, France, Germany, Italy, Luxemburg, the Netherlands) experienced a decrease in waste generation (Belgium and Netherlands) or a limited increase, ranging from around 1% (Germany) to around 8% (France).

In the first decade studied (1995–2005), there was a noticeable increasing trend of generated waste throughout Europe (the average variation was +9.57%), with marked trend differences among countries. While Germany decreased its waste generation by 9.3%, Malta increased it by more than 60%. Only five countries experienced a decreasing trend, all of which entered in the Union in 2004 (Slovenia, Lithuania, Hungary, and Slovakia) or 2007 (Bulgaria). Thus, all the European State members in 1995–2005 – with the Germany exception – experienced a growth in waste generation during that decade. In 1995, Germany was the EU country with the highest waste generation (623 kg per capita), while Greece was the country with the lowest generation (303 kg per capita).

Ten years later, in 2005, Denmark became the country with the highest waste generation, with an increase of waste generated per capita of 41%, while

Table 1.2. Municipal Waste Generated (kg per Capita) during 1995–2017 and Its Variations.

Country	EU Admission	1995	2000	2005	2007	2010	2015	2017	Var. 1995–2000	Var. 2000–2005	Var. 2005–2010	Var. 2010–2015	Var. 1995–2005	Var. 2005–2015	Var. 2007–2017	Var. 1995–2017
Denmark	1973	521	664	736	790		789	781	27.45%	10.84%			41.27%	7.20%	−1.14%	49.90%
Cyprus	2004	595	628	688	704	689	638	637	5.55%	9.55%	0.15%	−7.40%	15.63%	−7.27%	−9.52%	7.06%
Germany	1952	623	642	565	582	602	632	633	3.05%	−11.99%	6.55%	4.98%	−9.31%	11.86%	8.76%	1.61%
Luxembourg	1952	587	654	672	695	679	607	607	11.41%	2.75%	1.04%	−10.60%	14.48%	−9.67%	−12.66%	3.41%
Malta	2004	387	533	623	654	601	606	604	37.73%	16.89%	−3.53%	0.83%	60.98%	−2.73%	−7.65%	56.07%
Austria	1995	437	580	575	597	562	560	570	32.72%	−0.86%	−2.26%	−0.36%	31.58%	−2.61%	−4.52%	30.43%
France	1952	475	514	529	542	534	515	514	8.21%	2.92%	0.95%	−3.56%	11.37%	−2.65%	−5.17%	8.21%
Netherlands	1952	539	598	599	606	571	523	513	10.95%	0.17%	−4.67%	−8.41%	11.13%	−12.69%	−15.35%	−4.82%
Finland	1995	413	502	478	506	470	500	510	21.55%	−4.78%	−1.67%	6.38%	15.74%	4.60%	0.79%	23.49%
Greece	1981	303	412	442	453	532	488	504	35.97%	7.28%	20.36%	−8.27%	45.87%	10.41%	11.26%	66.34%
Italy	1952	454	509	546	557	547	486	489	12.11%	7.27%	0.18%	−11.15%	20.26%	−10.99%	−12.21%	7.71%
Portugal	1986	352	457	452	471	516	460	487	29.83%	−1.09%	14.16%	−10.85%	28.41%	1.77%	3.40%	38.35%
European Union – 28 countries		**470**	**521**	**515**	**523**	**504**	**480**	**486**	**10.85%**	**−1.15%**	**−2.14%**	**−4.76%**	**9.57%**	**−6.80%**	**−7.07%**	**3.40%**
Slovenia	2004	596	513	494	525	490	449	471	−13.93%	−3.70%	−0.81%	−8.37%	−17.11%	−9.11%	−10.29%	−20.97%
United Kingdom	1973	498	577	581	567	509	483	468	15.86%	0.69%	−12.39%	−5.11%	16.67%	−16.87%	−17.46%	−6.02%

Spain	1986	505	653	588	578	510	456	462	29.31%	−9.95%	−13.27%	−10.59%	16.44%	−22.45%	−20.07%	−8.51%
Lithuania	2004	426	365	387	419	404	448	455	−14.32%	6.03%	4.39%	10.89%	−9.15%	15.76%	8.59%	6.81%
Sweden	1995	386	428	477	486	439	447	452	10.88%	11.45%	−7.97%	1.82%	23.58%	−6.29%	−7.00%	17.10%
Latvia	2004	264	271	320	391	324	404	438	2.65%	18.08%	1.25%	24.69%	21.21%	26.25%	12.02%	65.91%
Bulgaria	2007	694	612	588	553	554	419	435	−11.82%	−3.92%	−5.78%	−24.37%	−15.27%	−28.74%	−21.34%	−37.32%
Croatia	2013		262	336	399	379	393	416		28.24%	12.80%	3.69%		16.96%	4.26%	
Belgium	1952	455	471	482	493	455	412	410	3.52%	2.34%	−5.60%	−9.45%	5.93%	−14.52%	−16.84%	−9.89%
Estonia	2004	371	453	433	449	305	359	390	22.10%	−4.42%	−29.56%	17.70%	16.71%	−17.09%	−13.14%	5.12%
Hungary	2004	460	446	461	457	403	377	385	−3.04%	3.36%	−12.58%	−6.45%	0.22%	−18.22%	−15.75%	−16.30%
Slovakia	2004	295	254	273	294	319	329	378	−13.90%	7.48%	16.85%	3.13%	−7.46%	20.51%	28.57%	28.14%
Czechia	2004	302	335	289	294	318	316	344	10.93%	−13.73%	10.03%	−0.63%	−4.30%	9.34%	17.01%	13.91%
Poland	2004	285	320	319	322	316	286	315	12.28%	−0.31%	−0.94%	−9.49%	11.93%	−10.34%	−2.17%	10.53%
Romania	2007	342	355	383	391	313	247	272	3.80%	7.89%	−18.28%	−21.09%	11.99%	−35.51%	−30.43%	−20.47%
Ireland	1973	512	599	731	772	624			16.99%	22.04%	−14.64%		42.77%			
Iceland		426	462	516	558	484	588	656	8.45%	11.69%	−6.20%	21.49%	21.13%	13.95%	17.56%	53.99%
Norway		624	613	426	491	469	422	748	−1.76%	−30.51%	10.09%	−10.02%	−31.73%	−0.94%	52.34%	19.87%
Switzerland		600	656	661	720	708	725	706	9.33%	0.76%	7.11%	2.40%	10.17%	9.68%	−1.94%	17.67%

Source: Our elaborations on Eurostat data, https://appsso.eurostat.ec.europa.eu/nui/submitViewTableAction.do

Greece remained the EU country with the lowest waste generation per capita, even if with an increase in the decade of 46%. In the following decade (2005–2015), with the entrance of new countries in the EU, the difference between highest and lowest waste generation per capita (Denmark and Romania, respectively) became more relevant, with a difference of 542 kg per capita recorded in 2015, and a decrease of 6.8% on average at EU-28 level.

In 2007–2017, waste generation at European level decreased by 7%, with only nine countries experiencing an increase in waste generation per capita, i.e., Germany, Finland, Greece, Portugal, Lithuania, Latvia, Croatia, Slovakia, and Czech Republic. The difference between best and worst country in terms of waste generation remained high, with more than 500 kg per capita of difference. Thus, EU experienced a marked decrease in waste generation, especially in the last years, although it increased its waste generation compared with that in 1995, with some countries experiencing a significant increase, such as Denmark, Malta, Latvia, and Greece.

Along with the analysis of European trends of municipal waste generation at both global and national level, it is of utmost importance to analyze the waste treatment trends, even if the European data considered the waste treated inside the EU, including imported waste and excluding the exported one, i.e., the amounts of waste treated are not comparable with the amounts of waste generated (Eurostat, 2019a).

Waste can be treated in different ways; it can be landfilled, incinerated (with or without energy recovery), recycled, or composted (Fig. 1.3).

As highlighted by EU data (Fig. 1.4 and Table 1.3), the development of waste treatment from 2004 to 2016 showed marked trends, with the landfill method reducing its relevance for EU waste treatment, decreasing 60% in terms of both total amount produced and kg per capita from 1995 to 2017.

The landfilling rate, which is measured considering landfilled waste as a share of generated waste, dropped from 64% in 1995 to 23% in 2017 in EU-28. This trend is particularly encouraging, as landfilling waste is considered the worst choice for environmental sustainability. By landfilling, material and energy resources from "waste" are completely lost. Moreover, without previous treatment, the environmental impact could be relevant and even permanent. Therefore, in accordance with the EU framework, waste landfilled should be limited as far as possible (Eurostat, 2019b).

To foster this goal, EU Directive 2018/850, amending Directive 1999/31/EC on the landfill of waste, requires that necessary measures are taken to ensure that *by 2035 the amount of municipal waste landfilled is reduced to 10 % or less of the total amount of municipal waste generated (by weight).*

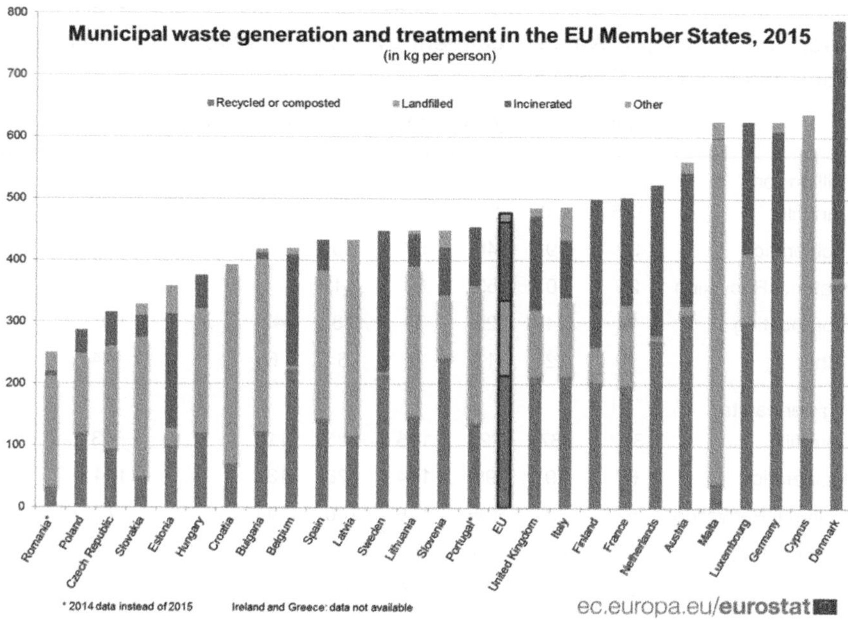

Source: Eurostat, 2017, http://ec.europa.eu/eurostat/documents/4187653/7825836/IMG+News+MW.png/9968509e-fada-4abd-8da6-a17e2ac21a2d?t=1485773088647

Fig. 1.3. Municipal Waste Generation and Treatment in the European Union (EU) Member States, 2015.

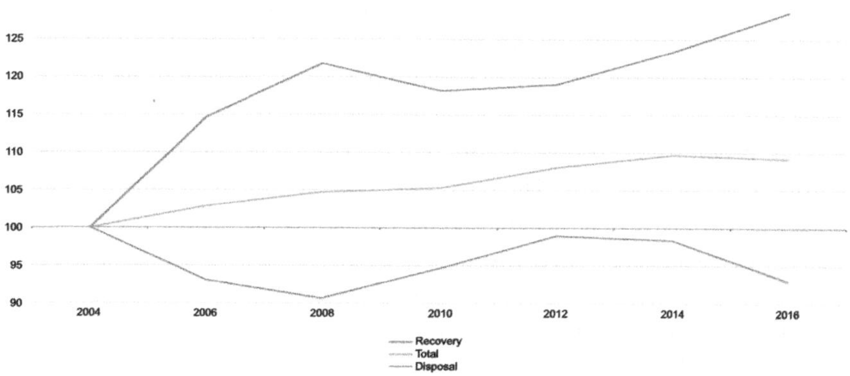

Source: Eurostat, https://ec.europa.eu/eurostat/statistics-explained/index.php/Waste_statistics#Waste_treatment

Fig. 1.4. Development of Waste Treatment, EU-28, 2004–2016.

Significantly, 80% of landfilled waste is represented by combustion wastes, household and similar wastes, and sorting residues (Eurostat, 2019b).

Table 1.3. Municipal Waste Treatment by Treatment Method, in Million Tons and in kg per Capita.[a]

	1995	2000	2005	2010	2015	2017	Change 1995/2017 (%)
Million tons							
Landfill	145	140	110	93	64	58	−60
Incineration	32	39	48	57	65	70	118
Material Recycling	25	40	52	63	71	74	195
Composting	14	24	29	34	38	42	196
Other	10	12	17	6	6	6	−44
Kg per capita							
Landfill	302	287	223	185	125	113	−63
Incineration	67	79	96	114	128	137	104
Material Recycling	52	83	105	126	140	144	177
Composting	29	48	58	67	75	81	179
Other	20	24	33	12	12	11	−45

[a]https://ec.europa.eu/eurostat/statistics-explained/images/5/5d/Municipal_waste_landfilled%2C_incinerated%2C_recycled_and_composted%2C_EU-28%2C_1995-2017.png

Source: Eurostat.

The EU Directive 2018/850 affirmed that landfill reduction *is necessary to prevent detrimental impacts on human health and the environment and to ensure that economically valuable waste materials are gradually and effectively recovered through proper waste management.*

This progressive process is fostered by the implementation of existing European legislation, e.g., Directive 62/1994 on packaging and packaging waste settled recovery targets that helped separately collecting the increasing amount of packaging waste. Moreover, Directive 31/1999 on landfill stated decreasing the maximum amount of biodegradable municipal waste to be landfilled, which fostered strategies to reduce the organic fraction of municipal waste to landfill.

As for waste generation, there were also several relevant differences across Member States in waste recycling and landfilling habits. EU data showed that some EU countries introduced landfill interdicts for recyclable, combustible, or untreated waste, and economic incentives to choose different treatment to divert waste from landfills. According to Eurostat, Netherlands, Belgium, Denmark, Luxembourg, and Sweden disposed of less than 10% of domestically generated waste in landfills (Eurostat, 2019b).

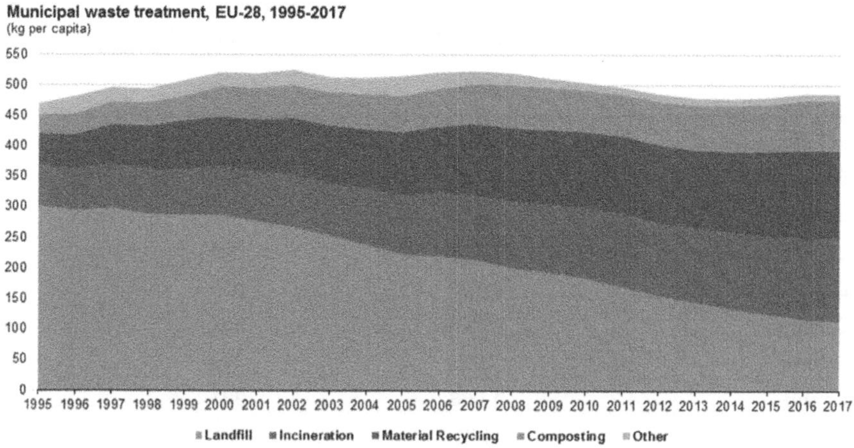

Source: Eurostat, https://ec.europa.eu/eurostat/statistics-explained/index.php/Waste_statistics#Waste_treatment

Fig. 1.5. Municipal Waste Treatment in the EU-28, from 1995 to 2017 (kg per Capita).

While landfilling of waste was the prevalent way of treating waste throughout Europe in 1995, during the following decades, incineration, recycling, and composting solution significantly increased their relevance from 1995 to 2017 (Fig. 1.5 and Table 1.4).

Recycling and composting increased the most and are the most sustainable practices, as they allow recovery of materials without or limiting the production of further waste such as that resulting from incineration processes (combustion wastes).

EU has largely progressed in fostering recycling activities. Although the recycling rate varied significantly among Member States, ranging from 78% in Belgium to 10% in Greece, 55% of domestically generated waste were recycled in the EU-28 in 2014.

However, as highlighted by EU, *in countries with a waste intensive energy production, the overall recycling rate is highly dependent on the management of the energy related waste types* (Eurostat, 2019b). Thus, policy decisions about how to treat waste at national, regional, and local level have an impact on the results obtained regarding the perspective and progresses achieved in the circular economy approach. Significantly, EU recently affirmed in the EU Directive 2018/850 *that reduction [of landfilling] should avoid the development of excessive capacity for the treatment of residual waste facilities, such as through energy recovery or low grade mechanical biological treatment of untreated municipal waste, as this could result in undermining the attainment of the Union's long-term preparing for re-use and recycling targets for*

Table 1.4. Incineration of Domestically Generated Waste, 2016.

	1,000 t	kg/inh	%
EU-28	138,619	273	18
Belgium	6,436	574	19
Bulgaria	221	31	1
Czech Republic	1,141	108	9
Denmark	3,129	555	36
Germany	45,096	557	32
Estonia	472	359	4
Ireland	1,068	231	23
Greece	142	13	1
Spain	3,751	81	7
France	19,373	293	22
Croatia	64	16	2
Italy	9,159	151	12
Cyprus	20	23	13
Latvia	142	71	7
Lithuania	112	39	5
Luxembourg	231	416	31
Hungary	1,357	137	13
Malta	7	17	2
Netherlands	11,432	677	25
Austria	3,260	381	26
Poland	6,068	160	8
Portugal	1,469	141	16
Romania	2,334	117	11
Slovenia	403	196	16
Slovakia	370	69	7
Finland	4,698	860	42
Sweden	6,526	673	40
United Kingdom	10,385	161	12

Source: Eurostat.

municipal waste as laid down in Directive 2008/98/EC. Similarly, while to prevent detrimental impacts on human health and the environment Member States should take all necessary measures to ensure that only waste that has been subject to treatment is landfilled, compliance with that obligation should not lead to the creation of overcapacities for the treatment of residual municipal waste (European Commission, 2018).

A relevant example is derived from Slovenia, which is the first European country with a "zero waste (ZW)" capital, Ljubljana, committed since 2014 with the goal of becoming a ZW city (Box 1.1). In a few years, Ljubljana significantly increased its recycling rate (from 29.3% in 2008 to the current 68%) and reduced by 80% the quantity of waste landfilled (Golob, 2019).

Ljubljana has been declared the European Green Capital for 2016. Among five finalists, *Ljubljana was the only one without an incineration plant nor a plan to build one, giving it a significant advantage over the other candidates. Even more this apparent disadvantage became an alternative solution that replaces disposal and energy recovery in the framework of a comprehensive waste management plan, namely the move toward a Zero waste society* (BiPRO/CRI, 2015).

Slovenia, through the publicly owned company JP Voka Snaga d.o.o. (a multiutility that manages the water and waste services for around 400,000 inhabitants in the City Municipality of Ljubljana and 10 other municipalities nearby), realized a project called "Upgrading of Regional Waste Management Centre Ljubljana (RCERO Ljubljana)" to improve and increase its waste management facilities, serving 37 municipalities in central Slovenia. The broad RCERO project contains three subprojects, i.e., a new landfill area, a treatment plant for leachate, and waste treatment facilities. As a result of the project, the amount of waste processed that is landfilled is now below 5%, while the rest is recycled as raw materials or as an energy source (Box 1.1).

Table 1.5 reports the percentages of waste treated using the recovery and disposal methods available in each Member State and at a global level (EU-28). The recovery methods are recycling, backfilling, and energy recovery, while landfill and incineration without energy recovery are considered disposal methods.

Along with countries that recover the great majority of waste generated (Belgium, Slovenia, and Italy), there are Member States with extremely high waste disposal rate (Greece, Bulgaria, Rumania, Sweden, and Finland). These data highlight again that there is low homogeneity throughout the EU about policies and strategies for waste management and that, without the adoption of strong measures to change route, the path for an effective European circular economy is still long.

From 1995 to 2018, landfilled municipal waste decreased by 61% (Table 1.6), while incineration, material recycling, and composting significantly increased. Although landfilling was predominant in 1995, it represented

Box 1.1

The Ljubljana Model: A Capital City Committed to the Zero Waste (ZW) Target.

EU affirmed that *as the EU steps up efforts to encourage the circular economy, cities across Europe need look no further than Ljubljana for inspiration on how to reduce waste and use resources in a smarter way* (European Commission, 2016). The Slovenian capital was declared 2016 European Green Capital, and it was the first European capital committed to achieving a ZW society *where products and resources are recycled or reused and almost nothing ends up in landfills. This is a remarkable achievement, accomplished over the past decade, in which policy-makers, businesses and citizens have worked together to create a more sustainable urban environment* (European Commission, 2016).

In describing the success of Ljubljana, EU stressed the fact that *among the five finalists for European Green Capital 2016, Ljubljana was the only city without a waste incineration plant or plans to build one. Instead, it focuses on alternative solutions, including a comprehensive waste-management plan that has made significant progress toward developing a zero waste society* (European Commission, 2016).

Ljubljana's publicly owned company, Voka Snaga, is the largest utility company in Slovenia, focusing on prevention, preparation for reuse, and recycling. It has a strategy that facilitates recycling and reuse, fosters separation and treatment, and encourages waste generation reduction, e.g., through a Center for Reuse directly managed in the center of Ljubljana. This center consists of a shop, sewing room, and workshop. Moreover, it has a Repair Café, where professionals, such as electricians or carpenters, are available for helping with repairs and transformation of the items. In four years since its establishment, the number of sold items increased from 50 to 190 per day. Further, in the shop, interested customers can buy local package-free bio cleaners, shampoos, several types of vinegar, and oil on a self-service vending machine, using only their own reusable packaging.

Moreover, Voka Snaga manages the Regional Center for Waste Management Ljubljana (RCERO), which is the largest cohesion fund environmental project, with a total investment of 155 million euros, and a good example of cooperation among municipalities to realize effectively circular economy. In 2006, seven Slovenian municipalities signed a cofinancing agreement, and nowadays, 58 Slovenian municipalities (with over 800,000 inhabitants) are involved in the project. This innovative plant, considered as the most modern waste treatment facility in Slovenia and Europe, was built on the existing landfill of Ljubljana and is made by waste treatment facilities, a wastewater treatment plant, and a new landfill. The plant construction began in 2014, and it was built in record time.

The mechanical–biological facilities for waste processing treat mixed household residual waste and waste from small business, service, and similar activities, along with separately collected biodegradable household waste. These plants have capacities of 150,000 and 21,000 t/year, respectively. Thus, RCERO processes a third of Slovenian waste with the crucial mission of extracting as much usable material as possible from mixed waste and separately converting collected biowaste into compost.

Residual waste is treated mechanically to extract usable materials for recycling or produce solid fuel. Biological waste is treated with anaerobic fermentation.

RCERO generates its own energy. As much as 95% of the seemingly useless mixed waste is processed into recyclable materials or fuel; less than 5% of residual waste ends up in a landfill.

In 2018, Ljubljana's separate collection rate was 68%, showing a sharp decrease in the quantity of residual waste produced.

Ljubljana and Voka Snaga ZW goals for 2025 are: (1) raising the recycling rate to 75% and (2) reducing the annual amount of residual waste per inhabitant to 60 kg.

only the third waste treatment choice in Europe in 2018, after material recycling and incineration.

Municipal waste treatment by incineration is particularly relevant in some EU countries, specifically the Nordic countries (Finland, Denmark, and Sweden), Germany, and Luxemburg, where over 30% of domestically generated waste were incinerated in 2014. In some countries, such as Finland, incineration is particularly high owing to the great amount of wood waste (80% of incinerated waste) (Eurostat, 2019b).

In Finland, landfill disposal of waste has ceased almost completely, as it covered around 0.7% of waste treated in 2018 (Fig. 1.6). This is partly because of law enforcement, with the landfill prohibition of organic waste in 2016 and an increase of energy recovery (Official Statistics of Finland, 2018). Indeed, energy recovery from waste with combined production of electricity and heat is the most significant treatment mode of municipal waste in Finland, covering 57%, with a slight decrease in the last years. Heat is particularly recovered in district heating networks. Moreover, along with energy recovery through incineration, Finland registered an increase in the amount of municipal waste generated per inhabitant and in the share of mixed waste. The most recent data available report that Finnish municipalities produced around 1.5 million tons of mixed waste, which increased over 20% relative to that in 2017 (Official Statistics of Finland, 2018).

The Helsinki Region Environmental Service Authority (HSY) outlined an ambitious target of a 60% recycling rate for municipal waste by the year 2025.

Table 1.5. Waste Treatment, 2016 (% of Total).

	Recovery			Disposal	
	Recycling	Backfilling	Energy Recovery	Landfill and Other	Incineration without Energy Recovery
EU-28	37.8	9.9	5.6	45.7	1
Belgium	76.9	0	12.6	6.4	4.1
Bulgaria	5.2	0	0.4	94.4	0
Czech Republic	49.5	29	4.5	16.6	0.4
Denmark	51.4	0	19.5	29.1	0
Germany	42.7	26.6	11.3	18.1	1.2
Estonia	21.6	11.2	2.5	64.7	0
Ireland	10.6	46	4.8	38.4	0.3
Greece	4.8	0	0.3	94.8	0
Spain	37.1	5.7	3.6	53.6	0
France	55	10.3	5.4	27.6	1.6
Croatia	47.2	4	1	47.8	0
Italy	78.9	0.1	4	14.2	2.7
Cyprus	10.4	28	3.8	57.8	0
Latvia	71.7	1.1	6.8	20.3	0
Lithuania	33.4	4.1	5.8	56.6	0
Luxembourg	34.8	24.2	2.1	39	0
Hungary	54.1	3.7	7.4	34.2	0.6
Malta	19.1	63.4	0	17.2	0.4
Netherlands	45.6	0	7.6	46	0.9
Austria	37	11		45.9	
Poland	46.2	22.2	3.3	28	0.4
Portugal	43.5	9.5	12.1	34.7	0.2
Romania	4	0.4	1.4	94.1	0.1
Slovenia	60.2	27.2	4.8	6.9	0.8
Slovakia	40	4.7	7	47.8	0.5
Finland	7.4	0	4.5	88	0
Sweden	12	4.9	6.6	76.3	0.2
United Kingdom	48.5	7.8	3.4	37.5	2.7

Source: Eurostat.

Table 1.6. Municipal Waste Landfilled, Incinerated, Recycled, and Composted in EU-28 during 1995–2018 (% of the Total Amount of Waste in Tons).

	1995	2005	2010	2015	2018	Change 2018/1995 (%)
Landfill	64%	43%	37%	26%	23%	−61
Incineration	14%	19%	23%	27%	28%	117
Material Recycling	11%	20%	25%	29%	30%	201
Composting	6%	11%	13%	16%	17%	202
Other	5%	6%	2%	3%	2%	−44

Source: Our elaboration on Eurostat data.

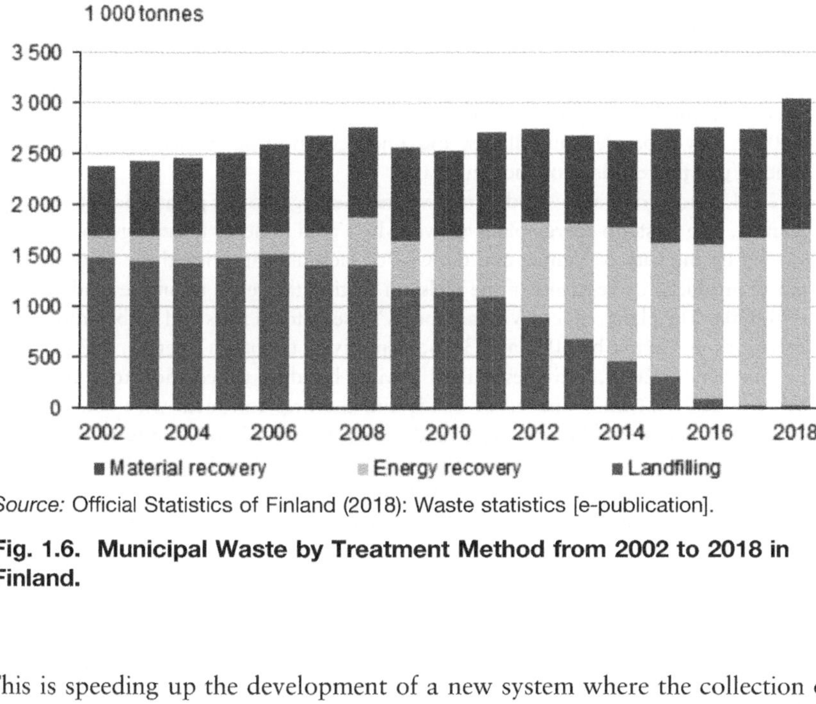

Source: Official Statistics of Finland (2018): Waste statistics [e-publication].

Fig. 1.6. Municipal Waste by Treatment Method from 2002 to 2018 in Finland.

This is speeding up the development of a new system where the collection of mixed waste is more expensive than that of other waste types. Indeed, a revision of the tariff system has been made and is under further development to encourage people to sort their waste and discourage them from just throwing it all in mixed waste (Box 1.2).

Box 1.2

Helsinki Region Environmental Services Authority (HSY) Waste Management Projects and Innovations in Last Years.

Helsinki Region Environmental Services Authority (HSY) is a municipal federation with Espoo, Helsinki, Kauniainen, and Vantaa as member cities. The municipal federation had around 764 employees involved in water and waste management activities in 2018.

In 2018, the recycling rate for homes was 48%, whereas the HSY target for 2025 is 60%. In accordance with its mission and strategy, HSY aims to *create the world's most sustainable urban region*. To reach this target, HSY wishes to be *at the cutting edge of environmental responsibility and resource efficiency, high reliability in performances, smoothly running services and a stable economy*. Indeed, HSY operated in self-sufficiency in energy and greenhouse gas emissions. The Helsinki Region Environmental Services Eco-Industrial Center (Ekomo) brings together actors in the circular economy sector who can benefit from each other's resources.

This center was built on the existing landfill opened in 1987. In 1993, biowaste treatment began, and the biowaste composting facility opened in 1997. In 2007, a new expanded landfill area and a new composting facility opened, and a landfill gas power plant opened in 2010.

In 2014, landfill operations ended, as a waste-to-energy power plant was opened in Vantaa. The waste-to-energy plant is owned by Vantaa Energy (an energy company owned by the City of Vantaa and the City of Helsinki); it reduced the amount of waste produced by residents of the Helsinki Region that ends up in the landfill by 374,000 t. The plant reduced Vantaa Energy's use of fossil fuels and carbon dioxide emissions in Vantaa by 40% and 30%, respectively (Vantaan Energia, 2020).

Further, in 2014, activities shifted toward building an ecoindustrial center, where biogas facilities opened in 2015, and the first contracts with businesses coming to operate in the area were made in 2016. Indeed, in Ekomo, companies can utilize others' waste and renewable energy generated in the area. In a circular economy approach, Ekomo aims to gather all kinds of players together to collaborate with each other and HSY. It wishes to represent a functional and high-quality basic infrastructure, with well-functioning data communication, connections, and road traffic network in the area. Further, it is relatively self-sufficient regarding energy.

Finally, a biogas power plant opened in 2017. It is publicly managed by the public body (HSY) that is also involved in waste collection services. It is the largest production plant for biogas in the Nordic countries.

In Ämmässuo ecoindustrial center, HSY:

- turns biowaste into biogas and soil products;
- treats ash and slag from the waste-to-energy plant;
- collects and utilizes landfill gas;

- treats contaminated soil extracts;
- sorts waste loads and forwards materials for reuse.

In 2019, the Ämmässuo ecoindustrial center received around 71,794 t of slag from the waste-to-energy plant and other waste to be processed, and around 94,000 and 14,777 t of biowaste and contaminated soil resources, respectively. It forwarded around 240,000 t of mixed waste from the Helsinki Metropolitan Area and Kirkkonummi to Vantaa Energy Ltd. for energy recovery. Moreover, Uudenmaan Woima Oy, a subsidiary of HSY, delivered around 90,000 t of mixed waste from nearby regions such as Nurmijärvi to the waste-to-energy plant.

The Ämmässuo ecoindustrial center, in operation since 2015, has a landfill site, biogas and composting plant for biowaste, landfill gas power plant, and a Sortti Station, which accepts small waste loads. In 2018, 473,000 customer visits were recorded at the five Sortti Stations managed by HSY, an increase of 7.7% compared to those of the previous year. In 2018, the Sortti Stations received 79,165 t of waste.

In the Helsinki area, landfill and incineration without energy recovery are almost eliminated as waste treatment alternatives. Recycling covered half of waste treatment, with energy recovery representing around 30% of waste treated.

1.2 THE CIRCULAR ECONOMY APPROACH

The circular economy model overcomes the traditional linear model to resource use. The linear approach is based on the idea that production of goods after the extraction of raw materials should be followed by the use and then by throwing away the used goods, transforming them into waste to be discarded (the approach is also known as "get – produce – use – throw"). Contrastingly, the circular economy approach aims at retaining the value of products, materials, and resources inside the "circle," by avoiding throwing away precious and scarce resources, instead using and reusing them as long as possible. According to the European Commission, *circular economy is a system where the value of products, materials and resources is maintained in the economy for as long as possible, and the generation of waste is minimised* (European Commission, 2015).

Ellen MacArthur Foundation (2015) defined it as *one that is restorative and regenerative by design and aims to keep products, components, and materials at their highest utility and value at all times, distinguishing between technical and biological cycles* (Ellen MacArthur Foundation, 2015).

This new approach allows to avoid the extraction of new resources and the production of unnecessary waste, which could endanger the environment and health in case of inappropriate management.

In 2018, Directive (EU) 2018/851, amending Directive 2008/98/EC on waste, stated: *Waste management in the Union should be improved and transformed into sustainable material management, with a view to protecting, preserving and improving the quality of the environment, protecting human health, ensuring prudent, efficient and rational utilisation of natural resources, promoting the principles of the circular economy, enhancing the use of renewable energy, increasing energy efficiency, reducing the dependence of the Union on imported resources, providing new economic opportunities and contributing to long-term competitiveness. In order to make the economy truly circular, it is necessary to take additional measures on sustainable production and consumption, by focusing on the whole life cycle of products in a way that preserves resources and closes the loop. The more efficient use of resources would also bring substantial net savings for Union businesses, public authorities and consumers, while reducing total annual greenhouse gas emissions.*

Circular economy is based on several steps involving all the actors of the economic system, from producers to end users, municipalities, waste utilities, and regulators. Indeed, in the circular economy framework, the product design should increase product durability, while allowing it to be easily repaired, upgraded, or remanufactured. Further, the production process should be resource-efficient and include recycled and reusable materials as components as much as possible. End users should be engaged in this new approach, sustaining and enforcing more sustainable behaviors, being conscious of their buying processes and consumption activities. Indeed, the circular economy framework *implies the adoption of cleaner production patterns at company level, an increase of producers and consumers responsibility and awareness, the use of renewable technologies and materials (wherever possible) as well as the adoption of suitable, clear and stable policies and tools* (Ghisellini, Cialani, & Ulgiati, 2016, p. 11). Therefore, it is a systematic approach that should encompass efforts by all the relevant stakeholders of economic systems, which mutually reinforce each other with virtuous behaviors and different styles of living, action, and innovation.

End users are a relevant part of a reuse and recycling approach, e.g., by separately collecting waste as in Ljubljana or using the existing recycling and reuse structures such as the Kretsloppsparken Alelyckan EcoPark in Gothenburg or ReTuna Park in Eskilstuna in Sweden, within a newly framed prevention, reuse, and recycle mindset.

Institutional actors, such as municipalities, could play a relevant role to foster the circular economy approach through their projects and their communication and engagement activities (Zapata & Zapata Campos, 2019).

Ljubljana launched a reuse center managed by a publicly owned company (Box 1.3), and a research project (project 6AIka Future Circular Economy Hubs in Finland – CircHubs) was undertaken in Finland to report the quantities of reuse and reuse-related business opportunities. One aim of CircHubs was to evaluate the quantities of selected products directed for reuse in

Finland's six largest city regions as well as nationally. Another interesting initiative by HSY was Petra Waste Benchmarking, which was a tool designed to follow up and estimate the amount of waste generated in companies and public organizations in relation to the number of personnel, turnover, and production volume. It could be used free of charge and helped to compare results with those of other operators in the same line of business, considering waste overproduction. Petra Waste Benchmarking also calculated greenhouse gas emission caused by waste, and its results could be used for environmental reporting.

The EU Sustainable Product Policy framework is based on three goals: designing sustainable products, empowering consumers and public buyers, and circularity in production processes.

Circular economy is viewed as a revolution that can increase not only environmental but also economic and social performance of firms and public institutions. Thus, looking into particular examples of circular economy is paramount. For example, the first plant to recycle nappies in Italy recently started, which can increase recycling of high-quality materials used for producing absorbent products previously treated as mixed waste.

Box 1.3

Innovative Solutions for Circular Economy in Ljubljana.

Voka Snaga in Ljubljana supports and encourages innovative solutions for a transition toward circular economy. Its model to foster effective waste management and circular economy is based on four pillars (Fig. 1.7): (1) legislation that should enforce recycling and reuse, along with responsibilities of households and users for good management of waste produced, e.g., since 2019, free plastic carrier bags are prohibited from all sales points in Slovenia; (2) control mechanisms to avoid free riding and wrongdoing, e.g., if waste is disposed improperly, Voka Snaga places a notification sticker on the bin, and if irregularities continue, the company will notify the municipality or intermunicipal inspectors who are responsible for oversight and issuing fines; (3) good service and infrastructures that allow to put into practice circular economy ideas and aims, such as the Regional Recycling Plant (RCERO) that realizes a virtuous recycling process, producing secondary materials, compost, and fuel, and significantly reducing landfill in Slovenia; (4) communication, which is essential to create awareness and foster proenvironmental behaviors and give citizens and users the knowledge to reduce waste produced and to realize an effective separate collection. A good example is *Snagazin*, a magazine provided once a year to all Voka Snaga customers, with information on good practices for waste management, information on the pay-as-you-throw (PAYT) tariff, articles, and interviews about reuse, recycling, and waste reduction practices.

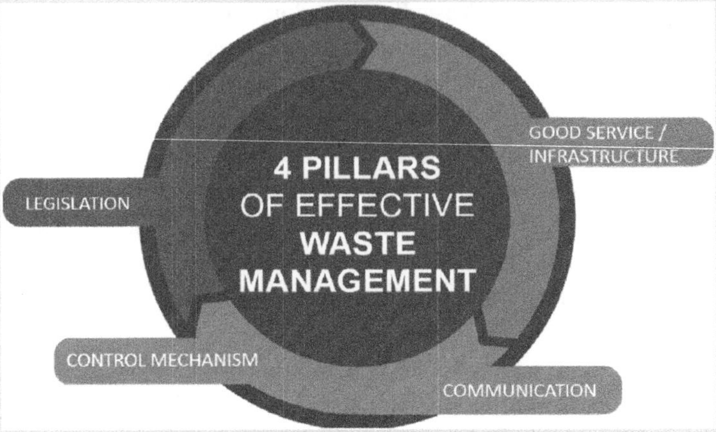

Source: Company Presentation, February 2020, provided by Voka Snaga

Fig. 1.7. Four Pillars of Good Waste Management for Voka Snaga Ljubljana.

Voka Snaga uses reused and recycled items as furniture in its offices, and cleans the city pavements with machines that recycle water and biodegradable detergent. Moreover, it has decided to stop using herbicides on public green and road surfaces. For street rinsing, mostly rainwater collected on the roofs of one of Voka Snaga building complexes is used.

In Ljubljana, waste prevention and waste separation is pursued at all public events (cultural, culinary, sports, etc.) with a system that is consistent, efficient, and user friendly. Further, Voka Snaga manages a Center of Reuse that sells on average 190 used items per day, and waste collection centers are available for free to all interested citizens.

Since 2015, RCERO can recover materials and energy from waste, in particular, producing 6,000 t/year of sorted secondary raw materials; 2,800 t/year of compost following the treatment of separately collected biodegradable waste, which has the highest possible quality and can be used on agricultural lands; 70,000 t/year of solid fuel from waste of different calorific values; 40,000 t/year of digestate; 13.400 MWh/year of electric energy, and 15,000 MWh/year of heat energy from biogas produced in the process.

The separate collection and PAYT tariff method have been in place for several years, and citizens are aware of their responsibilities in waste management. Since 2006, Voka Snaga has collected biowaste door-to-door for households, and this collection method was extended to other recyclables (paper, glass, plastic) and residual waste in 2013. For residual waste, the frequency of collection was reduced to foster waste separation. In the city center of the Capital City (Ljubljana), 69 underground collection units replaced almost 9,000 bins for effective and esthetic waste disposal.

The PAYT tariff is calculated only considering unsorted residual waste and organic biological waste, and the other waste fractions are covered through the extended producer responsibility rule. Unsorted and organic waste costs are accounted depending on the bin size and monthly emptying frequency. Tariffs for multiresidential buildings depend on the size and number of bins, bin collection monthly frequency, and the number of household members or that of building tenants. In these cases (multiresidential buildings), the building's manager usually receives the bill and then divides it on the basis of law or agreements among tenants.

Households pay 9.85 € per month on average, among the lowest prices in Slovenia. Paper, metal, and batteries are sold by Voka Snaga, and revenues are used to lower tariffs.

Door-to-door and PAYT tariffs are demonstrated to be effective in increasing separately collected waste and reducing the amount of residual waste produced (Fig. 1.8), making Ljubljana the EU capital with the highest share of recycled waste.

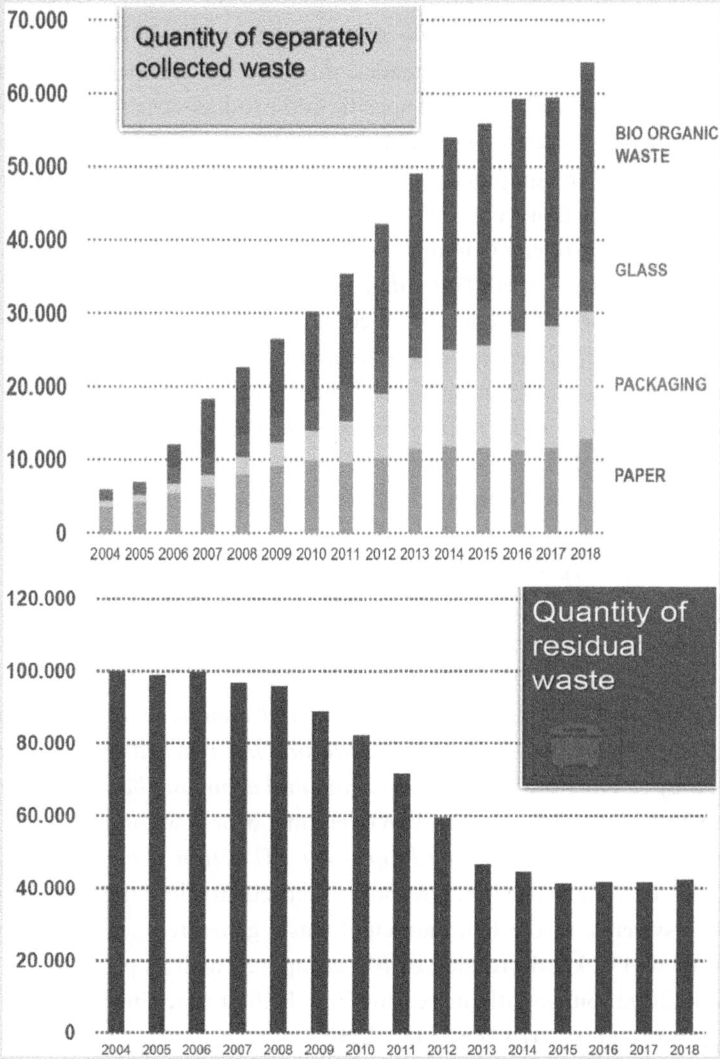

Source: Company Presentation, February 2020, provided by Voka Snaga

Fig. 1.8. Separate Collection and Residual Waste Production Results from 2004 to 2018.

The EU circular economy approval measures began with the German experience (Davis & Hall, 2006), and today, circular economy is considered as the next major European political economy project (McKinsey & Company, 2015), with the European Commission launching the so-called European Green Deal to drive and manage a sustainable green transition as a new growth strategy, including, among others, sustainable solutions to preserve the environment and act in a climate-neutral manner.

Starting from the 90s, the EU amended its 1975 Directive on waste management twice: in 1991, the EU firmly established the "reduce, reuse, recycle" priorities, and in 1996, two more amendments to the 1975 Directive were promulgated. Along with the amended directive that created the EU framework, there are other EU material-specific and product-specific directives, such as the packaging directive (Directive 94/62/EC), the directive on waste electrical and electronic equipment (Directive 2012/19/EU), and the directive on end-of-life vehicles (Directive 2000/53/EC).

In 2014, the European Commission released a communication (COM2014 398) on this topic, named *Towards a circular economy: A zero waste programme for Europe*. The concept of circular economy can be described as a *new way of creating value, and ultimately prosperity, through extending product lifespan and relocating waste from the end of the supply chain to the beginning – in effect, using resources more efficiently by using them more than once* (UNIDO, 2017).

The communication of the European Commission (European Commission, 2014b) affirmed that *moving towards a more circular economy is essential to deliver the resource efficiency agenda established under the Europe 2020 Strategy for smart, sustainable and inclusive growth. Higher and sustained improvements of resource efficiency performance are within reach and can bring major economic benefits. Circular economy systems keep the added value in products for as long as possible and eliminates waste. They keep resources within the economy when a product has reached the end of its life, so that they can be productively used again and again and hence create further value*. This communication was then overcome by a new communication with an evocative name: *Closing the loop – An EU action plan for the Circular Economy*. Turning waste into a resource is crucial to close the loop in circular economy systems. In the EU, municipal waste generated per person in 2015 amounted to 477 kg, decreasing by 9% compared with its peak of 527 kg per person in 2002, but slightly increasing, for the first time since 2007, from the 474 kg recorded in 2014 (Eurostat, 2017).

In March 2020, the European Commission adopted a new Circular Economy Action Plan (European Commission, 2020a), considered one of the main elements of the Europe's new agenda for sustainable growth: the European Green Deal.

Although substantial progress has been made in promoting sustainable ways of waste management in Europe, the launch of the new plan was needed owing to the consideration that the European economy is *still mostly linear, with only 12% of secondary materials and resources being brought back into the economy. Many products break down too easily, cannot be reused, repaired or recycled, or are made for single use only. There is a huge potential to be exploited both for businesses and consumers* (European Commission, 2020a).

According to McKinsey & Company (2015), Europe lost 95% of the material and energy value, while material recycling and waste-based energy recovery captured only 5% of the original raw material value. Thus, the opportunities of a circular economy approach are plenty: *circular economy, enabled by the technology revolution, allows Europe to grow resource productivity by up to 3 percent annually. This would generate a primary resource benefit of as much as €0.6 trillion per year by 2030 to Europe's economies. In addition, it would generate €1.2 trillion in non-resource and externality benefits, bringing the annual total benefits to around €1.8 trillion versus today* (McKinsey & Company, 2015, p. 12). It has been estimated that a circular economy could induce a GDP increase of as much as 7% relative to the current development scenario. Moreover, circular economy could be a positive employment opportunity (McKinsey & Company, 2015).

An Italian institutional report further affirmed that by 2030, circular economy will have the potential to create between 1.2 and 3 million jobs in Europe and to reduce the unemployed citizens from a minimum of 250,000 to a maximum of 520,000 units (Senato Della Repubblica, 2016).

This encouraging data have been further confirmed, as the European Commission reported how a *recent study estimates that applying circular economy principles across the EU economy has the potential to increase EU GDP by an additional 0.5% by 2030 creating around 700 000 new jobs* (Cambridge Econometrics, Trinomics, and ICF, 2018; European Commission, 2020a).

Therefore, circular economy is paramount for EU policy, which aims to develop a sustainable economy. The circular economy framework includes the key EU priorities such as jobs and growth, the investment agenda, climate and energy, the social agenda and industrial innovation, and global efforts on sustainable development. Peter Lacy and Jakob Rutqvist significantly affirmed: *Transitioning to the circular economy may be the biggest revolution and opportunity for how we organize production and consumption in our global economy in 250 years* (Lacy & Rutqvist, 2015).

1.3 THE ZERO WASTE STRATEGY FOR MUNICIPALITIES THROUGHOUT THE WORLD

The ZW framework (Connett, 2013) considers waste as a potential resource with value to be realized, rather than as a problem to be dealt with, and this value lies in adopting the circular economy approach. At the expiration of their lives, goods are reused, repaired, sold, or redistributed within the system. Additionally, if reuse or repairs are not possible, products can be recycled or recovered from the waste stream and used as inputs by other operators, replacing the demand for extraction of natural resources. Thus, the same materials are used again and again, so that no materials are wasted or underused.

According to Connett (2013), the ZW strategy *says no to incinerators, no to mega landfills, no to the throwaway society, and yes to a sustainable society* (Connett, 2013, p. 9). In the intent of the author, ZW is a new direction for society not only for the economy, i.e., a vision and a path to follow to reach a real sustainable way of living.

Indeed, the European Investment Bank decided to refrain from financing the municipal waste incinerator in Belgrade, Serbia, in 2019, by highlighting that incinerators tend to crowd out waste prevention and recycling measures (CEE Bankwatch Network, 2019). Even the EU worried about the negative outcomes of waste energy production on recycling activities (Eurostat, 2019b).

For example, data about the Helsinki area, where a new incineration plant was commissioned in 2014, showed that MSW generation increased, and recycling rate did not increase significantly, remaining lower than 50% of household waste (Fig. 1.9).

ZW cities would recycle all their waste or recover all possible resources from waste streams and produce no harmful waste for the environment (Zaman & Lehmann, 2011).

Throughout the world, in the United States and Europe, several municipalities have adopted a ZW strategy following the pioneering examples of San Francisco in California and Capannori in Tuscany.

As reported by Connett (2013), the case of San Francisco demonstrated that, by applying "the First Five Steps" to ZW (among the total 10 steps), it is possible to reach a diversion rate from landfill of 80%, a higher rate than that reached by building an incinerator (which allowed a reduction of 75% by weight, as the remaining 25% is ash still to be treated). These first five steps are: (1) source separation, (2) door-to-door collection systems, (3) composting, (4) recycling, and (5) reuse, repair, and deconstruction.

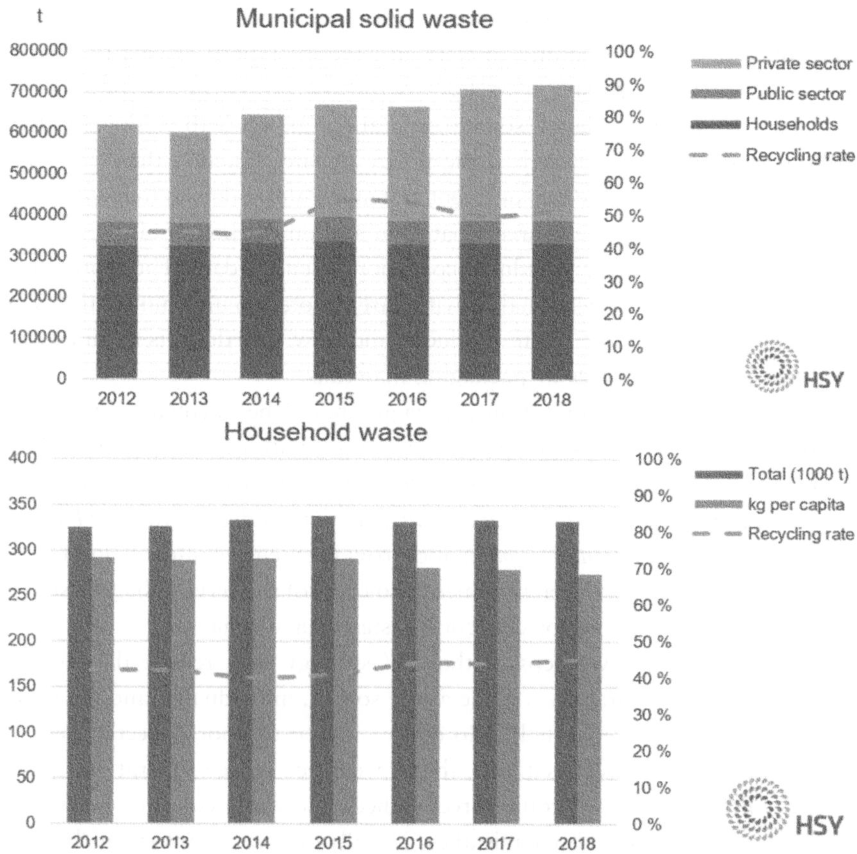

Source: https://www.hsy.fi/en/experts/climatechange/Pages/circular-economy.aspx

Fig. 1.9. Waste Generation and Recycling Rate in Helsinki Region.

Separate collection of recycling materials is required by the European legislation, i.e., the Waste Framework Directive, adopted on November 19, 2008 and then revised, specifies percentages for recycling paper, glass, metal, plastics, and nonhazardous construction and demolition waste. Moreover, and increasingly important, source separation and door-to-door collection systems together can make households and all waste system users aware of the quantity and quality of waste produced, at least on a weekly basis. This awareness helped to identify systems to reduce this production by changing lifestyles.

In fact, the possibility to confer the waste produced each day at all times realized an unsustainable situation where households did not know exactly how many bags of plastic containers have been used and thrown away during the week. Contrastingly, by accumulation of the waste produced in the house, terrace, or garden, it is possible to be aware of the exact amount of packaging and total waste produced and to start an awareness path driving to a more conscious buying and using lifestyle.

This educational role of source separation along with a door-to-door collection system is neglected in the policy debate. Usually, their introduction in a municipal waste management system creates a debate focused on the difficulties of appropriate source separation and on the households' problems to retain waste until the scheduled collection calendar date. Therefore, most communication and educational activities are devoted to informing citizens on how to best separate the waste produced and how to reduce its volume, e.g., by pressing plastic bottles or packaging materials.

However, a deep information campaign should be devoted to informing citizens on the awareness role of these activities, with question such as *Were you aware of how much waste you produced in only a week? Now you are! If you multiply this volume for the weeks in a year and a decade you can have an idea of your environmental impact*, and provide extensive information on the reduction of impact to the environment and costs of the service that the source separation and door-to-door collection systems have achieved.

In fact, the first two steps of the ZW strategy may reduce the costs of recycling (as the separation is made at the source, individually, and the waste collected is already separated). Moreover, a door-to-door collection system can contribute to educate citizens about a correct source separation, as the waste collection operator could directly check the waste collected every time and inform each user about mistakes. Usually, waste operators in door-to-door collection systems should not collect incorrectly prepared waste bags or containers. During the start-up period, they should inform citizens with a ticket about their mistakes (for example, by posting a red ticket on the bag or a message such as "this bag has not been collected because of wrong source separation"). Thus, citizens are corrected each time and introduced to an accurate source separation.

A good quality of recycling material is strictly linked not only to effective recycling but also to selling opportunities, and thus, revenues for waste utilities to reduce tariffs for recycling firms or consortia. No black bags are allowed in the ZW system, and each bag should be relatively transparent to allow this check by operators and to avoid users making mistakes without realizing. As suggested by Rossano Ercolini, who was awarded the 2013 Goldman Environmental Prize (Ercolini, 2018), the black bag for unsorted waste should be avoided and opened up by all interested stakeholders to assess how much unsorted waste is generated by wrong source separation and how much are goods that have been wrongly designed, projected, and constructed. These goods should be avoided by customers in their consumption habits and, most importantly, should be redesigned by producers to make them sustainable and appealing for conscious consumers. Therefore, both source separation and door-to-door collection systems, i.e., the first two steps of the ZW strategy, should be introduced not only to increase composting and recycling but also to foster citizens' awareness and engagement about their waste production and how to best reduce the waste volume and composition, avoiding goods that are not compostable or recyclable.

Further, composting is a step before, and thus more important, than recycling, as the quantity of organic waste produced by households is higher than that of other dry wastes and causes odor and leachate and methane production in landfills. The San Francisco example showed that it is possible to send kitchen and other organic waste to a composting plant located in an appropriate place, e.g., 100 km away from the city but surrounded by farmlands, which uses the compost produced by the plant. This choice allowed the municipality and waste utility to create value from organic waste by transforming it into valuable compost (Connett, 2013). The example of RCERO in Ljubljana is outstanding. A plant built on the old landfill that transforms organic waste into first quality compost to be sold to farmers and interested citizens and that produces almost no odor owing to its technology.

Along with the first five steps, there are five other relevant steps in the ZW strategy, i.e., (6) waste reduction initiatives, (7) economic incentives, (8) residual separation and research facilities, (9) better industrial design, and (10) interim landfills (Box 1.4).

The waste reduction initiative could be introduced at local and national level, aimed at fostering the attention of good practices such as the use of reusable bags or reusable materials. Thus, local or national regulators could introduce taxes on the use of plastic bags or other plastic or unsustainable materials such as single-use packaging, introduce and encourage shops or supermarkets that allow to recharge bottles or other containers, or ban plastic and disposable materials from schools, sport competitions or fairs, or other events.

In Ljubljana, Gothenburg or Capannori (Box 1.5), the publicly owned waste utility or the municipality created and managed reuse centers that also sell unpackaged goods, thus supporting the creation of shop opportunities for recharging products such as soaps, shampoo, beverages, milk, etc.

Economic incentives are mainly possible through tariff systems that effectively encourage good waste management, including appropriate sorting activities at household level and more sustainable consumption habits. On this matter, ZW policies encourage the introduction of PAYT tariffs, which allow each household to pay not only on the basis of family size or house dimension but also on the basis of the appropriate waste management practices, so that each community member pays on the basis of how much waste is thrown away (polluter pays principle) (BiPRO/CRI, 2015).

As highlighted by Marques, Simões, and Pinto (2018), *Pay-as-You-Throw systems are relevant to change users/citizens habits …, while the financial sustainability of the utilities is assured* (Marques et al., 2018, p. 292). These tariff systems have been applied for several years in different contexts and are spreading rapidly, owing to the support of local and national authorities.

Box 1.4

ASCIT Spa, Capannori, Italy: a pioneer in the Italian ZW strategy

ASCIT Spa was established in 2004 and carries out its activity in the field of collection and disposal of solid urban and similar waste in six municipalities in Tuscany, Italy (Altopascio, Capannori, Monte Carlo, Pescaglia, Porcari, and Villa Basilica), by means of direct contract. The company serves a catchment area of over 80,000 inhabitants and over 32,000 families in the plain of Lucca. Four of the six municipalities served by ASCIT are part of an important paper and tissue district, one of the most important at national and European level. In their territory, there was a strong activist movement fighting against the building of an incinerator and in favor of the closure of the existing one in the 90s.

The "ASCIT model" has become a subject of study at national and international level over time, with delegations from other municipalities and even geographically distant countries, such as Tunisia and Brazil, interested in visiting the company and enhancing their choices by replicating them in other contexts.

In 2005, ASCIT pioneered the door-to-door collection in the municipality of Capannori, the largest of the municipalities served. In 2007, for the first time in Italy, the Capannori administration adopted the ZW strategy in collaboration with ASCIT, imagining waste as a resource and projecting the municipality toward a goal of progressive waste reduction until its elimination by 2020. Thus, the municipal council formally adopted the first Italian resolution to adhere to the ZW strategy in 2007.

At the end of 2018, ASCIT recorded a turnover of 15.5 million euros, with 144 employees, and a vehicle fleet of 149 units, without treatment or pretreatment facilities.

Therefore, the municipality of Capannori was the pioneer of the ZW strategy in Italy. In September 2019, 291 municipalities in Italy (6.5 million people) have adhered to this strategy through a formal resolution adopted by the City Council. The formal adhesion through town council decision is important as, after that, it is more difficult to change the ZW path, e.g., owing to a change of mayor or the City Council composition. In fact, another contrary decision should be assumed by the City Council, considering the possible impact and reaction of environmental activists and all citizens.

ASCIT has extended the door-to-door collection service throughout the territory of the municipalities served since 2010. In particular, in two municipalities, Porcari and Villa Basilica, the door-to-door service has been extended to the whole territory. In the other municipalities, the complete coverage, with the elimination of the collection with road bins took place in 2010, and finally in Pescaglia in 2015, also extending to the most isolated areas, where proximity bins were installed.

In recent years, the company has extensively implemented some significant innovations in the service management and particularly, the following was introduced in all municipalities in 2013:

- Door-to-door collection of the light multimaterial, with separate collection of glass every two weeks;
- Door-to-door collection of plastic crockery, always within the light multimaterial collection service;
- Home collection of used vegetable oil on a daily basis without prior notice;
- Door-to-door collection of pruning and leaf waste (active only in the municipality of Capannori, on payment and at the request of the user).

In 2011, the first reuse center called DACCAPO was inaugurated, which is a solidarity reuse center that currently has two locations, where it is possible to donate objects to have them repaired, transformed, and allocated to those who still need them. The DACCAPO Reuse Center is known on the initiative of the Diocesan Caritas of Lucca and the Association Ascolta La Mia Voce Onlus, in collaboration with the Municipality of Lucca, Municipality of Capannori, Sistema Ambiente, and ASCIT.

The center creation was inspired by virtuous initiatives developed in some European countries and, in particular, by considering Swedish reuse centers such as that of Kretsloppsparken in Gothenburg.

The preparation of a reuse center allows to achieve several objectives: (1) reduce the operator's commitment to collect bulky items at home, lowering the cost of the service; (2) make citizens aware of the "nonwaste" and reduction of waste produced, as some goods that are no longer useful to a citizen can instead be useful to other citizens or still be converted to other uses with an intervention by the employees center; finally, (3) generate a new market in solidarity, which can give new life to objects that can be made available to people and families in need, increasing the social cohesion of citizenship.

In the two active centers in the municipalities served by ASCIT, you can find not only home accessories, furniture, clothes, footwear, children's items, but also artifacts produced with recycled materials during the workshops organized.

In 2012, punctual pricing was started experimentally, which then became definitive in 2013. After 2013, analyses were carried out on the operating methods for carrying out waste collection services and to map the territory of the municipalities served, with the aim of proposing and implementing improvements at the request of citizens, such as the separate collection of diapers and greenery, the double weekly collection of multimaterial, also considering services for nondomestic users involved in the door-to-door collection.

For all municipalities served by ASCIT in 2019, the share of collected waste has decreased by over 800 t, due to a substantial reduction of assimilated and bulky waste to be distributed. The share of separate waste collection stood at over 72%, considerably above the regional and national averages of 53.88% and 55.52%, respectively.

The results obtained in these years confirm ASCIT as a reference business model, not only at national level.

Residual separation and research facilities are fundamental steps in the ZW strategies, and they are considered effective in waste reduction and redesigning stakeholder enforcement to producers. As highlighted by Connett, *the former attempts to make the residuals disappear, the latter sets out to make them very visible* (Connett, 2013). Residual separation facilities help to reduce residual waste by allowing to correct mistakes in separate collection through effective separation of residual waste and waste that can be further recycled after separation, e.g., the impact of RCERO in Ljubljana demonstrated the ability of such facilities to foster recycling. Further, research facilities are useful to understand what and how many errors occur in product design and packaging choices from producers. Moreover, they help to understand the most frequent errors in separate collection to foster communication and education campaigns, making them more effective. It is relevant that research centers communicate directly with waste operators to support them with their knowledge.

For example, Contarina in the Veneto Region realized a deep analysis of its mixed waste to understand the relevance of different materials included in mixed waste and their evolution over time. The analysis showed that the most relevant products treated as mixed waste were absorbent products (27% and 29% of mixed waste in 2016 and 2015, respectively). This information should encourage firms to find better solutions to recycle the most relevant sources of mixed waste. Indeed, Contarina collaborated with Fater SpA to realize the first plant to recycle absorbent products by obtaining precious secondary raw materials and reducing mixed waste.

Box 1.5

The Project of the ZW Research Center of Capannori.

The Project of the Municipality of Capannori in Tuscany, *Concrete steps towards Zero Waste,* included the establishment of a ZW Research and Redesign Center, which analyzes the residual waste of the municipality. It has the essential purpose of identifying the type of materials, objects, and/or items still present in the unsorted waste of the municipality. Once the residual flows have been identified, the research center works by: (1) improving the separate collection level, avoiding the "improper contributions" in unsorted waste (e.g., organic fractions, paper materials, plastics, glass, etc.), which entails a better communication with citizens (in collaboration with ASCIT) to maximize separate collection; (2) regarding those objects and/or items that are currently neither recyclable nor compostable or that are difficult to recycle, such as disposable razors, coffee pods, and, more generally, "disposable" products, "polymaterials" such as the tetra pak, blisters, and several types of plastics starting from the shoppers, the ZW Research Center will begin an industrial redesign process of this "criticality" identified items and will contact the producer requiring the manufacturer's extended liability on the basis of a detailed proposal. Finally, (3) the project, in close collaboration with ASCIT and the municipality, puts in place initiatives aimed at reducing waste at source through its "waste reduction counter," spreading the positive experiences of the EFFECORTA store (tap products, bulk products etc.) and contributing to the spread of reusable diapers.

Furthermore, the project aims at locally creating a recycling and composting supply chain and promoting repair and reuse centers by the valorization of materials collected through separate collection, giving a "second life" to used goods. Finally, the project will survey the "best practices" at national and international level with the aim of taking them on and making them well-known.

As of today, the center has realized several national and international collaborations, while participating in research projects. It has also developed several initiatives to foster redesign activities with multiple producers, such as changing coffee pods into compostable ones with disposable coffee pod producers.

The ninth step is "Better Industrial Design," i.e., adopting instruments to force producers to design their products in a sustainable manner, making them recyclable, reusable, and without planned obsolescence. On this matter, the recent new Circular Economy Action Plan launched in March 2020 by the European Commission reported that *up to 80% of products' environmental impacts are determined at the design phase* (European Commission, 2020b).

The Commission highlighted the need, among others, to improve product durability, reusability, upgradability, and reparability, increase recycled content in products, restrict single-use products, ban the destruction of unsold durable goods, and reward products based on their different sustainability performance, also through incentives for high performance in terms of durability and reparability (European Commission, 2020b). Moreover, the European Commission stressed the relevant role of public procurement: *Public authorities' purchasing power represents 14% of EU GDP and can serve as a powerful driver of the demand for sustainable products* (European Commission, 2020b). For these reasons, focused attention to this step of the ZW strategy is expected in Europe in the next few years.

The last step of the ZW strategy is "interim landfill." Landfills should be progressively eliminated in the ZW strategy because of the goal to achieve ZW. A landfill should be considered as a transitory place to dispose of what cannot be reduced, reused, recycled, composted, or redesigned (Connett, 2013). The example of Ljubljana is again relevant here. Through several instruments (door-to-door collection, PAYT systems, communication and education plans, and technological innovations in waste treatment and recycling), only 5% of unsorted waste is landfilled, requiring a new landfill, only for treated not biodegradable waste, which is expected to last decades.

In the ZW strategy, what enters the landfill needs to be controlled to avoid toxic or biodegradable materials. This control activity will prevent a dangerous impact for the environment and health, and allow having a direct track record of the content of landfills to manage them in accordance with best sustainable practices.

2

ZERO WASTE GENEALOGY: A SOCIAL MOVEMENT AND THE ITALIAN EXPERIENCE[1]

ABSTRACT

The chapter will describe the genealogy of the international social movement "Zero Waste (ZW)" and highlights its role of cultural, organizational, and scientific reference point for the waste management, in particular the public one in Italy. The chapter proposes to interpret ZW as a part of a wider social movement on "common goods" that in Italy proposed a radical critics of the neoliberal governance of local public services. The climax of this movement was the referendum of 2011, when 27 millions of Italian citizens voted against the privatization of waste, water, and transport management at an urban level. By door-to-door recycling, composting of community, pay as you throw system (PAYT), reuse centers, and environmental communication, ZW movement succeeded to create an apparatus of driver concepts for the management of waste. In particular, some of the proposed case studies were the actors that implemented the ZW strategy findings on the territory, experimenting new organizational and social practices aimed at increasing recycle and at converting the local economy into a circular one.

Keywords: Zero waste; knowledge management; cultural hegemony; circular economy; collaborative networks; take–make–waste

We set two objectives in this chapter: (1) to carry out a genealogy of the zero waste (ZW) strategy, i.e., to reconstruct the main arguments and events that generated this discourse and made it, progressively, increasingly capable of questioning the hegemony of traditional waste management systems based on

---

1 This chapter was written by Claudio Marciano.

large disposal and road collection plants; (2) to focus on the processes of knowledge exchange between the different social actors involved in the ZW vision, often characterized by an implicit and nonformalized dimension.

ZW is a discourse with a strong symbolic apparatus, starting from its very name. However, it also has an organizational and technological apparatus, which is made explicit through various implementing devices, including door-to-door differentiated waste collection, Pay as you throw (PAYT) tariffs, community composting, reuse centers, and the marked rejection of incineration plants and landfills to recover urban waste.

Our main hypothesis is that, although today, ZW is at the center of the strategies of important waste utilities, this is the result of an elaboration conducted in an original context of knowledge exchange, in which different forms of capital have circulated (Bourdieu, 1992) between social movements, universities, local administrations, and municipalized companies.

Not a single ZW practice was born with the aim of strengthening profits, nor as the result of a technological process. In the ZW vision, the efficiency of waste collection and treatment systems depends largely on the involvement of the population and is measured by performance indicators such as the percentage of separate collection or the amount of waste produced on average by a household, which is ecologically rather than economically relevant.

The hypothesis of ZW being a field of managerial as well as social innovation reinforced the fact that almost all the successful experiences described in these pages relate to special companies or companies with completely publicly owned capital. These companies do not aim to produce profits and are characterized by greater territorial responsibility than a private entity.

Therefore, ZW stands as the thematic outpost of a broader idea of converting the economy and cultural logic that has dominated the management of local public services in the neoliberal sense over the last 20 years (Brenner, Marcuse, & Maier, 2012; Harvey, 2011) and crosses with the political discourse on common goods, particularly in the Italian experience.

2.1 THINKING ZERO WASTE SOCIOLOGICALLY

In the introduction, we referred to some concepts such as cultural hegemony, genealogy, and social movement, which have rarely been approached by the ZW movement, but are strategic in understanding how this phenomenon originated and spread.

The concept of cultural hegemony is linked to the political and philosophical thought of Antonio Gramsci, who elaborated it in the notebooks written from prison. However, it has crossed the interdisciplinary reflection on the relationship between culture and power until today (Said, 1978), fascinating authors of different theoretical matrices, well beyond the boundaries of Marxist doctrine (Baratta, 2006; Hall, 1981).

Gramsci uses the concept of cultural hegemony to describe the ability of the dominant class to direct the mentality, lifestyles, and languages of the subordinate ones, thus consolidating and stabilizing its supremacy on a consensual basis (Vacca & Rossi, 2007). It would succeed in this essentially because, although living in the working condition is a factor of mutual recognition, the subordinate classes would not have developed their own weltanschauung, i.e., worldview, and would tend to internalize the value system of the dominant one (Lears, 1985).

Cultural hegemony means that an intimate bond is consolidated between managers and managees, and a common interpretation of reality is shared. However, it also means that this bond can be broken, and that alternative narratives can be consolidated and more credible.

Cultural hegemony is also established in the field of waste management.

Waste collection and treatment systems incorporate a precise vision of social relations and cultural values in their technological and economic devices. Road collections, conducted with large vehicles capable of emptying bins that are always accessible, imply a model of blasé citizenship, in which participation essentially consists of paying taxes, and in which social control over delivery is very limited. These systems also propose a service economy in which the main surpluses occur in disposal activities, which are by definition capital intensive. In contrast, separate waste collection is conducted with smaller vehicles, is labor intensive, and balances the economic weight of the service more closely with collection, making waste treatment a potentially profitable activity for the transferor. The social contract that inspires these systems is based on a strong sense of responsibility on the part of citizens, who are entrusted with the task of correctly sorting and displaying waste and paying the fee according to their consumption behavior.

In proposing a new waste management system, ZW also proposes a new model of citizenship and a different, if not contrasting, apparatus of values and social representations to those of traditional management systems.

However, where did the idea of separating waste and activating recycling chains come from? Why, at a certain point and only for a part of the population, have landfills and incinerators been considered dangerous for communities? To understand how ZW has deconstructed the cultural hegemony of traditional collection systems and propagate an idea of efficiency and reliability with respect to its organizational proposals, it is necessary to consider a genealogical view.

Similar to the concept of cultural hegemony, the concept of genealogy has characterized the reflection of power in the social sciences for decades. However, it was the philosopher Michel Foucault who used the concept of genealogy as a method of historical-social investigation. Genealogy is an approach that attempts to reconstruct how some discourses have become hegemonic compared to others. It showcases the history of power, understood as the ability to direct cultural and, therefore, economic processes in a certain direction.

In our case, the ZW strategy was created to counteract the use of landfills and incinerators as the preferred industrial solution for waste disposal. It has progressively consolidated itself as an apparatus composed of technological ideas and models of social organization derived from research carried out in the fields of industrial ecology, bioeconomy, and urban metabolism (Zaman & Ashan, 2019). With its operational success and based on the regeneration of value from waste, it has inspired a broader idea of converting the economy from linear to fossil-driven to circular. Today, this idea runs through the arena of global environmental policies from Europe to the United States and South America.

Who animates ZW? Who are the social actors generating and disseminating its contents? The answers to these questions require referring to a deeply consolidated theoretical component in contemporary sociology on social movements (Castells, 1997; Della Porta & Diani, 2020; Touraine, 1978).

ZW is, in fact, a social movement, and as all movements, it grasps and denounces anomalies in the dominant system, is spread by an elite of experts endowed with relevant cognitive and symbolic capital and within itself, and its elements operate through very diversified action structures (Marciano & Montani, 2012). A movement can be instantial or systemic, depending on the type of objective it sets itself; it can adopt confrontational or lobbying practices, depending on the type of relationship it intends to have with the institutions. The movement can be bureaucratized and established as an informal network, or both organizational solutions can be observed within the movement itself.

In the next section, in the light of this theoretical premise, we try to reconstruct the arguments, events, and social actors that generated the ZW model on a global level.

2.2 TAKE–MAKE–WASTE VERSUS ZERO WASTE

To describe the scenario that generates ZW as a social movement, it may be useful to start from the definition of its antagonist model, which is defined "take–make–waste" or TMW in critical academic work (Mazzarella, Escobar-Tello, & Mitchell, 2016).

2.2.1 Linear Waste Cycle

Historically, the waste cycle has been shaped by the economic and cultural assumptions of the linear economy. The adjective "linear" is what the theorists of the circular economy (Ghisellini, Cialani, & Ulgiati, 2016) have attributed to the dominant economic paradigm based on (1) the intensive use of fossil fuels, (2) the extraction of raw materials, and (3) an expected demand for goods constantly growing (Bonomi, Della Puppa, & Masiero, 2017; Marciano, 2017).

In the TMW model, the role of the main cleaner in the production process is played by the landfill and/or incineration plant. Waste value is primarily economic and is calculated using a formula that subtracts the potential returns of recovery from the disposal costs (Massarutto, 2011).[2]

Since the 1960s, landfill disposal has established itself in advanced capitalist countries and has emerged as a low-cost solution for the absorption of the first large quantities of municipal solid waste (Pietzsch, Duarte Ribeiro, & de Medeiros, 2017). With the exponential progression of the quantity of goods consumed and the change in quality of waste to be disposed of (more plastic and electronic waste), a landfill has become a less profitable and socially accepted solution than incineration, as the latter also guarantees energy recovery and the possibility of recovering material downstream of the collection processes.

Over time, landfills and incinerators have proven to be integrated solutions, i.e., waste from incineration requires a service landfill to be disposed of, and have based their business models on a medium-long plant life cycle (over 20 years) and the scalarity in the ratio between investment cost and energy yield, e.g., a small incinerator (20 W) can cost about 40 million euros and about seven million euros in annual operating costs, while a large incinerator (280 MW) can cost about 270 million euros and have operating costs of about 60 million euros (Iaboni & De Stefanis, 2007).

The collection model interdependent to these plants is that of street bin collection, which is a preferential choice in some urban and especially metropolitan contexts, where a vertical urban planning and a complexity of services (residential, commercial, tourist) require simplified collection systems.

TMW supporters have highlighted the strengths of this system and the weaknesses of the possible "adversary," i.e., ZW. In particular, on

2 VR = (CRD + CT − PR) - (CIND + CS), where VR is the value of a certain material, CRD is the cost of separate collection, CT is the cost of treatment activities aimed at recovery downstream of separate collection, PR is the market price of the recovered material, CIND is the cost of undifferentiated collection, and CS is the cost of undifferentiated disposal.

reconstructing a small part of the scientific literature evaluating collection systems (Massarutto, 2011), the following arguments emerge recurrently: (1) separate collection and recycling chain costs are too high, and returns are too low to manage the entire volume of waste produced in urban contexts; (2) separate collection, even door-to-door, does not completely eliminate waste, and produces it in turn, given the need to clean and refine the secondary raw material to make it salable; (3) technological developments have considerably limited the environmental risk of incineration plants and landfills themselves; (4) secondary raw materials, derived from separate collection, are often destined to developing countries, which, however, purchase these materials less and less, such as China, or have very little domestic regulation, such as African countries; (5) the raw materials used for the production of municipal solid waste would not have scarcity problems, i.e., sand for glass, cellulose for paper, and for plastic, the same would require a minimum percentage (0.5%) compared to oil consumption for other purposes; (6) automation, present in large road collection vehicles and incineration plants, makes the space gap between worker and waste increasingly wide, reducing accidents at work and also the executive load. In contrast, door-to-door collection would reduce this "emancipation" and would be exhausting for workers, given the need to "get on and off" the vehicle, especially in the case of single-operator vehicles.

In the TMW model, separate collection and waste reduction policies are considered compensatory, but not exclusive, instruments of efficient waste management. It is significant that the ZW concept is used by international organizations, such as the International Solid Waste Association and the Solid Waste Association of North America, as an attribute of incineration plants. This would help to eliminate the residual fraction not absorbed by the recycling chain.

Data confirm that the TMW model is currently dominant: only 15% of the total waste produced is recycled, while the remaining 85% is divided between incinerators and landfills. In addition, the amount of waste annually produced tends to increase, with World Bank projections forecasting a doubling of the annual amount produced (about 1.5 billion tons) by 2050 (World Bank, 2017). However, these data differ across continents, e.g., in the European Union (EU), separate collection is 40% (Eurostat, 2017).

2.2.2 Circular Waste Cycle

However, the TMW model has long been subject to criticism, starting from its theoretical premises and the technological devices that incorporate them.

First, there is extensive literature that highlights the weaknesses of both landfill and incineration plant systems (Connett, 2013; Dansero, Putilli, & Tacco, 2015; Zaman & Ashan, 2019). In particular, the criticisms on incinerators concern several aspects: (1) the considerable environmental impact, owing to the atmospheric particulate matter that they release during the combustion process and the poor possibility of verifying the efficiency of the filtering systems; (2) the disincentive to push separate waste collection beyond a certain level, as the plants need undifferentiated waste in constant quantities to operate and be economically supported; (3) having investment costs that are too high and too long term, making radical innovations impossible in the short term; (4) energy production would be extremely low compared to that of incineration, and its economic importance would be entirely dependent on public finance.[3]

These criticisms, mainly made by experts linked to the ZW movement, are reinforced by a series of alternative proposals to make the waste cycle cheaper and more sustainable. Unlike the supporters of TMW, those of the ZW model do not consider incinerators and separate collection as complementary practices, but as alternatives, to the extent that waste separation is followed by other waste disposal practices.

The ZW vision has been reconstructed by several authors (Bratina et al., 2016; Curran & Williams, 2012; Leo & Salvia, 2017) whose analyses tend to coincide on some arguments that constitute the conceptual basis on which ZW is based.

The cultural root of the ZW model is the same that inspires circular economy: nature is a ZW system where any resource is regenerated, and following its model, a transition must be set up that overturns the current paradigm based on the extraction of raw materials and the production of waste.

ZW general principles are as follows: (1) waste is a resource; (2) a waste management system is efficient if it aims to completely eliminate waste; (3) the development of public policy guidelines should guide the design of products and services; (4) communication is a key investment resource to strengthen public participation and awareness; (5) the green supply chains that can develop in the separate collection market are conducive to new employment;

3 In Italy, since 1992, there has been an incentive (defined CIP6: Comitato Interministeriale dei Prezzi) that assimilates the production of energy from incinerators to that derived from renewable sources, establishing a real artificial market. This has allowed those who operate an incinerator to sell the energy obtained from the combustion process at a price approximately three times higher than that of energy production using conventional sources for a long period of time.

(6) the life cycle of products must be longer, and planned obsolescence must be abolished; (7) investment in technology and research is needed to improve landfill remediation processes.

From these principles, 10 steps were derived toward ZW described in 1.3., which summarize, in an effective communication formula, part of the most important devices of the ZW model: (1) organization of separate collection systems; (2) adoption of door-to-door collection systems with containers separated by type of waste; (3) creation of plants capable of transforming organic waste into compost; (4) creation of plant platforms for recycling and recovery of materials; (5) adoption of active policies for the "upstream" reduction of waste, from domestic and community composting to the promotion of tap water instead of packaged waste; (6) creation of centers for the reuse and repair of durable goods, from clothes and furniture to household appliances; (7) adoption of point pricing systems based on the PAYT principle; (8) construction of plants for the recovery of nonrecyclable, special, and industrial waste; (9) establishment of research centers and redesign of goods and services according to the circular economy model; (10) achievement of ZW within a certain period.

At a global level, the ZW vision is conveyed by a number of networks where scientists, journalists, policymakers, and local activists converge. The ZW International Alliance (ZWIA) is a global platform that has organized annual meetings since 2002 to exchange knowledge and share successful practices in applying the ZW vision at the local level. It was created as part of an international conference on waste management by a community of academics and political activists. Through ZWIA, the ZW movement has institutionalized the identity of communities and businesses that want to recognize themselves in its principles, as demonstrated by the two certifications issued by the network to local businesses and communities.

Another network particularly focused on mobilizing and supporting local grassroots is the Global Alliance for Incinerators Alternatives (GAIA). The alliance is made up of approximately 800 formal and informal associations distributed on all continents, which share the objective of combating the practice of waste incineration, as it is risky for human health and uneconomical. GAIA has engaged in supporting grassroots and sometimes local public administrations, environmental conflicts to prevent the construction of incinerators and landfills in different parts of the world, e.g., in Mexico, where local communities around the large city of Acapulco have opposed and prevented the construction of four mega plants, or in the United States, where the local ZW movement in Detroit has put in place several comparative practices against the local incinerator, one of the largest worldwide.

Among the associations responsible for spreading the ZW philosophy on a continental, national, and territorial level, ZW Europe (ZWE), founded in 2009, networks municipalities, companies, universities, and environmental associations from over 30 European countries. ZWE is among the stakeholders involved by the European Parliament in the elaboration of directives on circular economy, and several of its experts, in collaboration with those of GAIA and ZWIA, are a reference point for the elaboration of waste management policies at continental level.

Neither GAIA nor ZWIA have ever bureaucratized membership of their networks or set up administrative structures, while ZWE and, in general, the national and transnational sections of ZW decided to adopt a different strategy, equipping themselves with their own staff and encouraging a constantly mobilized voluntary network.

The archipelago of structures that incorporate and spread the ZW vision has the same characteristics of heterogeneity and plurality described in the sociological literature about environmental movements (Marciano & Montani, 2012). Formal and informal structures coexist, so that waste management is only a tool for the expression of an ecological vision of social relations or a specific theme of action and adopts practices of lobbying toward institutions or debate and knowledge exchange with universities and companies, or on the contrary, are more specifically expressed in practices of confrontation, mobilization, and conflict, such as the grassroots movement constituted against incinerators and landfills.

The Italian case represents this plurality, where (1) ZW is the reference discourse of important municipal, provincial, and regional administrations; (2) the network of associations and structures that identify with its model are scattered throughout the territory; and (3) both the oppositional nature of ZW with respect to the TMW model and the intense practices of knowledge exchange between the social movement and companies responsible for waste collection and disposal management emerge strongly.

2.3 ZERO WASTE IN ITALY

Italy is one of the countries where the ZW movement has spread the most and where its action to raise awareness of citizenship has been most successful, which is demonstrated by some data. In 2017, separate collection in Italy was among the first in Europe with an average of 55%. If only the most populous countries on the continent are taken into consideration, Italy is second, just a few steps away from Germany (60%). In addition, it has the best performance in per capita waste production, recording much lower values than those of all other European countries with comparable economies (Eurostat, 2019a, 2019b).

To explain how ZW is rooted in Italy, we must refer to two conditions typical of the national context.

The first is the historical and acknowledged penetration of organized crime in the management of municipal solid waste (Cianciullo & Fontana, 2005). This area has been, and still is, among the most problematic in terms of collusion between politics and malfeasance, with thousands of Eco-Crime or Eco Offenses registered by the Italian judiciary every year (Ganapini, 2004).

The second, often a direct consequence of the first, is that the major Italian cities (Rome, Naples, Milan) have been affected by dramatic crises in waste management, with streets and squares turned into landfills for days.

These phenomena, undoubtedly depressing, have, however, proved to be enabling the activation of resilient and strongly reforming energies, both at local and national level. Waste management in Italy has become a field of innovative practices, aimed at achieving positive environmental results, but also strengthened by an ethical profile, with a deeper political significance than the ecological dimension tout court.

As in any complex social process, it is difficult to establish a starting point. Moreover, as we set ourselves the goal of focusing on knowledge exchange processes, it is necessary to note that these have been achieved mainly tacitly, rather than explicitly (Dyer, Gregersen, & Christensen, 2011; Nonaka, 1991). Long before ZW was established as a discourse, its contents were already formulated in the Italian political and social debate, spread by intellectuals and ecological journalists (Conti, 1988; Nebbia, 1990). It was only at the end of the 1990s that the first systematic elaborations arrived with reference to the ZW strategy (Tornavacca & Onida, 1999).

However, ZW was mainly spread by public events of great media impact, and microphysics of initiatives spread throughout the territory and aimed at showing the possibility of an alternative to the traditional TMW system.

2.3.1 Milan: From Crisis to Model

The waste crisis in the city of Milan in 1995 was undoubtedly one of the most significant events that allowed to ZW theories to have an immediate practical expendability and a strong media resonance.

In 1995, Milan was served by the Cerro Maggiore landfill, where it delivered 97% of its waste daily. For years, the local population disputed over the closure of the plant, which had reached saturation point, subject to continuous extensions of dubious legitimacy by the region and investigations by the judiciary about environmental damage.

In October 1995, the citizens of Cerro organized roadblocks because the Lombardy region decided to extend the landfill's life cycle for another two years. An institutional crisis opened up, which blocked waste collection in the whole metropolitan area of Milan, where up to 30,000 tons of garbage remained on the streets (Ganapini, 2004).

However, the crisis activated a very innovative organizational response in an extraordinarily short time, which would inspire waste management in several cities, Italian and European, for the following years. Particularly, we can note some steps that the Milanese experience implemented for the first time. These will become consolidated steps for the management and communication of ZW.

In the years when these experiences took hold, the hegemonic discourse on waste management was unconditionally that of TMW, in which landfills and incinerators were the heart of the system. In the municipal utilities of large Italian cities, often owners of disposal plants, and in the technical departments of universities, often called upon to design public planning where investments in incinerators and landfills are legitimate, the idea of setting up collection systems on technologies and organizational models such as ZW is considered utopian. This vision, only in part, would be institutionally challenged by the approval of the Ronchi Decree (Legislative Decree 22/1997), which would set the ambitious goal of 65% separate collection to be achieved in the national territory.

Because of the waste on the streets, the first action of the City Council of Milan and its Municipal Administration (Azienda Milanese Servizi Municipali (AMSA)) was to reach an agreement with the neighboring Emilia-Romagna Region, which offered the availability of its plants (landfills and incinerators) to dispose Milanese waste for a few months.

In that short period of time – about three months – AMSA organized a mechanical–biological treatment plant, with a capacity of about 2,000 t/day, in a disused industrial site owned by Maserati. The plant was built in record time by a consortium formed by the Gruppo Finanziario Lombardo, the owner of the area, and four leading companies in the waste sector such as the German company RWE, the American multinational BFI, and the Italian companies Sorain Cecchini and Daneco, employing about 100 workers from the former Falck (Pagni, 2002).

The total investment was about 80 million euros, and the price per kg guaranteed by the plant was about 100,000 lire/t – less than half the cost of disposal at the Cerro landfill. At the same time, the municipality started door-to-door separate collection, including the organic fraction, and was the first city in Europe of that size to adopt such a radical system. Milan adopted systems that had already been tried and tested in Germany and Holland on a much smaller scale.

For the first time, it was experimented with small-capacity vehicles, which, therefore, had a lower portability than the three-four-axle models of the road collection, but a greater capacity for reaching and mobility in Milan's metropolitan contexts.

The plan implemented by Milan was supplemented by the opening of two "Riciclerie," ecological islands dedicated to the recovery of bulky waste, which will inspire the Centers for Reuse promoted by the ZW movement. The establishment of a Civic Forum was fundamental to the success of the experience, led by journalist and writer Guido Viale, which brought together Milan's civil society in a shared project to raise awareness of citizenship. The system allowed to achieve 35% differentiation, a remarkably high percentage for the time. Despite not always constant trends (the separate collection of organic waste was not definitively activated until 2014), Milan is currently the city with the highest recycling percentage by number of inhabitants in Europe, perhaps in the world, recording a percentage of 60% in 2018.

The Milanese experience is also significant because it acted as an incubator for the expertise that will consolidate ZW in Italy, both in management and communication.

An example is the "Scuola Agraria del Parco di Monza" (Agrarian School of Monza Park), a public research institution founded in 1920, which promotes training and culture in various fields, including the design of waste separation and composting systems. In 1993, the School designed one of the first door-to-door differentiated waste collection systems in the small town of Bellusco, a few kilometers from Milan. In a few days, it reached 65% separate waste collection, mainly owing to the separation of organic waste, in a local context such as Lombardy, where regional regulations, in particular Law 21/1993, provided for targets of less than 25%.

In the wake of the success of Bellusco, the School organized monthly meetings and seminars at its headquarters, involving those who began to practice the ZW experiences from below, even before they were so defined.

In this way, a community of practices was formed that combined scientific approach and concrete application in the territories and developed a real "heresy" in waste management.

Therefore, the Agrarian School of Monza Park became the forge of an increasingly recognized expertise, which included, as structured researchers or consultants, Enzo Favoino, Attilio Tornavacca, Massimo Centemoro, and

Raphael Rossi, who would be called in different institutional contexts to put into practice the ZW guidelines. In particular, the School became the reference point for dozens of municipal administrations, which decided to entrust it with the design of the urban hygiene service, or for various provincial and regional administrations, such as those of Turin and Milan, which entrusted it with the task of drawing up the plans for the waste systems. It also became a processing platform for important innovations in the field of both industrial and community composting, which would form the basis of future Italian and European regulations on the subject.

2.3.2 Good Practices and Collaborative Networks

Thanks to these experiences and to the first publications that systematized ZW practices (Tornavacca & Onida, 1999); an intense dialog between local political actors and ZW expertise was born in the second half of the 1990s and, to a greater extent, in the new millennium.

This dialog is based on successful experiences in cities that are increasingly important considering their size and urban complexity. The most effective tool for raising awareness became the exposition of good practices. Seminars, conferences, and to a greater extent, company visits were organized, through which the technological and organizational devices tested in the field to implement the ZW vision were disseminated among chains of local administrators and managers of management companies. The aim was not only to standardize collection and processing practices but also to recognize the existence of interdisciplinary expertise capable of implementing ZW in any territorial area. Among the most relevant examples of this relational model is the experience of Contarina. Contarina is a company with total public capital, which operates in a territory of about 50 municipalities, almost entirely covering the Province of Treviso in the Veneto Region, serving about 554,000 inhabitants, with a turnover of almost 80 million euros in 2018, and a net profit of 1.2 million euros. The company is responsible for the entire waste cycle in these territories, where it deals with both separate waste collection and treatment and disposal (See Box 3.6).

In 1997, Contarina introduced door-to-door recycling in an area where undifferentiated road collection was carried out. Only two types of household collection were envisaged, i.e., dry and organic, while plastic and paper were collected in bins on the road. To facilitate the separation of wet waste, Contarina provided users with a perforated tub smaller than the bin where the waste had to be placed for road exposure, aiming at facilitating the aeration of the container and limit unpleasant odors, as well as accustoming citizens to set their waste production in a reduced volume. Contarina technicians, among which the figure of Paolo Contò stands out, noticed that there was a correlation between the quantity of waste produced and the volume of the bin used to collect it, i.e., more space supply was equivalent to greater demand. This small innovation, together with the reduction of the undifferentiated waste collection shifts (from three to two times a week), contributed to the achievement of extraordinary results in a short time, on a large and densely populated area.

Recently, Contarina exposed a new method to make the PAYT system even more efficient, the so-called "Quadrinomy," which introduces additional variables, such as the volume of the bins used by the household, and the inclusion in the calculation of the punctual fee for emptying the workforce and other waste that constitutes a cost in the treatment processes.

Contarina spa has a spin-off, also with completely public capital, called Sintesi Srl, which designs waste collection systems and company industrial plans. Dozens of municipalities and public companies have used its professionalism to set up an efficient collection system. Recently, through an innovative tool for public governance, namely a "Cooperation Agreement," Contarina was hired to manage the start-up of Alea Ambiente, a company that has been set up by the municipality of Forli and by more than 12 municipalities of the Romagna hinterland.

Contarina, in the imagination of ZW Italia, has an idealistic role. However, it is not the only reality to be exported as an efficient management model. Another important pole, both for the innovations introduced and for the visibility obtained in the ZW circuit, is that of Capannori.

Capannori is a municipality in the Province of Lucca, with about 45,000 inhabitants, where one of the most important cellulose industrial districts in Europe is located. Here, the Region of Tuscany decided to set up an incinerator in 1994. However, the project would be blocked by an extraordinary mobilization of local civil society.

The Capannori Municipality was among the first to join the international ZW network, adopting a resolution in the City Council with the commitment to implement the "10 steps" established by ZWIA. Over the years, it was followed by other 300 institutions in Italy and Europe. The declared objective is to go beyond the deserving experiences of separate waste collection, already established in Italy for years, and to specialize in innovative practices of waste reduction and prevention.

The service is managed by a public company, ASCIT, which serves five other municipalities in the area (see also Box 3.1). It is, therefore, confirmed, also in this experience, the greater functionality and flexibility of a public governance in the adoption of organizational and technological systems, such as punctual pricing, which have an opposite objective to TMW, i.e., to reduce, and not increase, the demand for waste treatment.

Capannori implements PAYT, as Contarina and other Italian experiences, but it also introduces new initiatives, including a regulation for waste tax, by which operators who adopt containers on tap or introduce small innovations in product packaging are rewarded. The municipality also raises awareness among large companies, such as Lavazza, to produce coffee capsules with recyclable materials, and to spread the use of washable nappies, by taxing the families who buy them. Moreover, in Capannori, two reuse centers were inaugurated, along the lines of the Milanese experience, where bulky waste is delivered and reprocessed to recover reusable materials.

However, perhaps the most distinctive element of Capannori's experience is the sensitivity toward the production of shared knowledge on the ZW theme and the creation of an extraterritorial network of partnerships with other municipalities, as well as public and private companies interested in joining the community.

The establishment of the National ZW Observatory is exemplary of Italian ZW. The Observatory has set up a research center on waste management, with focus on the composition of dry waste and nonrecyclable fractions, to reorient production design and raise awareness among families and companies of the need to adopt behaviors consistent with a circular vision of the economy. The Observatory is also the reference point for the Italian ZW network, to which about 300 local administrations have joined to date, meeting annually to share training and knowledge shared in their local practices.

Moreover, in this experience, charismatic figures such as Rossano Ercolini and Alessio Ciacci have played an important role in the activation of knowledge exchange networks. Both of them have exported the Capannori experience and the systematization of the ZW discourse in hundreds of debates, meetings, seminars, and visits outside their own territory. The former, an elementary teacher and a militant environmentalist historian, was awarded the Goldman Prize for his political activity and nonfiction production, while the latter, environmental councilor at Capannori and administrator of public companies in the environmental field was awarded in 2012 as Personaggio Ambiente Italia.

In Capannori's experience, the analytical element with which we opened this chapter is even more evident, i.e., that innovation in the organizational and technological field of the ZW discourse is the result of a horizontal interaction between social movement, research, politics, and business world. Another case in which ZW practices, public service management, and wide symbolic resonance of the experience coincide is that of Ponte nelle Alpi, in the

Province of Belluno. Unlike Contarina and Capannori, in this experience, the manager, an in-house company, does not have a critical mass of tens or hundreds of thousands of inhabitants, but a single territory with less than 10,000 inhabitants. Additionally, in Ponte as in Capannori, the spread of the ZW political and cultural discourse was affirmed well before the ZW concept itself was coined and as a consequence of a project by the Province of Belluno to set up a landfill in the territory. The grassroots movement was created to oppose the plant; it turned into a civic list and won the local elections, appointing Ezio Orzes, a local environmentalist, as the environmental councilor. Therefore, the local administration decided to set up an in-house company and extended door-to-door recycling to the whole city. Ponte's objectives were the same as those set out by Formia in 2013, i.e., to demonstrate that public management can be more efficient than private management and, at the same time, to guarantee the government of the territory to citizens without delegating private subjects to industrial roles with public purposes. Ponte, from an organizational point of view, was inspired by the experience of Contarina, already an advanced leader of ZW in Italy in the early 2000s. After over 70% of recycling in the first few months, Ponte introduced punctual pricing, reaching over 90% differentiation, one of the highest levels of waste regeneration ever recorded in Italy and Europe.

2.3.3 ZW and Social Innovation Networks: ERICA, the Recycling Municipalities, the Virtuous Municipalities Association

To understand how the ZW framework was established in Italy, it is useful to analyze the experience of ERICA, a cooperative established in the 90s in the territory of Alba, Province of Asti. Here, a social movement was constituted in the form of an enterprise, although it has simultaneously maintained a political and social purpose.

ERICA was founded in 1996, after the dramatic flood of the Tanaro river in 1994, which affected 70 victims and caused enormous economic damage to the provinces of Alba, Asti, and Alessandria. The cooperative aims to implement good environmental practices in the territory, including the separate collection of waste. Its founder, Roberto Cavallo, a biologist and environmentalist, was appointed Councilor in Alba in 1997. In the same year, drawing on the experience already underway in Milan and particularly at the Consorzio dei Navigli, he introduced door-to-door differentiated waste collection in his city. Although with some small variations in the intensity of collection calendars, the model implemented in terms of the means of collection and the organization of work is the same of Milan. The standardization of these steps allowed ERICA to export the Albese model to other municipalities in the area, including the small town of Villafranca d'Asti (3,000 inhabitants), where it was possible to reach 85% separate collection and reduce the amount of waste per capita to less than 50 kg at the beginning of the century.

In those years, the partnership between ERICA and Capannori was born, which would be inspired by the Piedmontese solutions to implement the innovations previously described in its territory. The relational network that today constitutes the strategic infrastructure of ZW Italia was consolidated in these moments (debates, events, twinning, sit in case of environmental disputes). Additionally, ERICA is the leader of a project financed with EU funds, called "Re.Re" (Reduce and Recycle). The project involves the formation of a network of municipalities that practice ZW. In the network, there is one municipality where ERICA designed the collection system, Dogliani, but this was also done in other cities of France and Spain, spreading waste reduction practices abroad. These include dual labeling for packaging, the spread of washable nappies, campaigns for the use of tap water, and domestic composting.

ERICA, as an entrepreneurial subject, adheres to the Charter of Naples. This is an important document that should be mentioned with a view to define the outlines of a complex and dynamic process such as the diffusion of ZW in Italy.

The Charter of Naples was promulgated in 2009, when a dramatic waste crisis was underway in the Neapolitan city. ZWIA organized one of its international dialogs in the Neapolitan city in collaboration with the ZW networks already consolidated in Italy. The Charter aimed to establish the identity boundaries of the ZW movement and to raise the attention of the various levels of government involved in the resolution of the waste crisis in Naples. It is no coincidence that, a few years later, the local municipalized company manager in Turin, Raphael Rossi, would be called to manage one of the most representative figures of the ZW movement in Italy.

Finally, in this overview, we cannot overlook the circuit of the Recycling Municipalities of Legambiente. This is an annual initiative organized by the most widespread national environmental association, in which data on waste collection in Italian municipalities are compared. The "recycling" municipalities are those that exceed 65% of separate waste collection. There are also more detailed categories, such as the municipalities that obtain the best results on domestic composting or waste reduction. The initiative is accompanied, every year, by an award ceremony and the release of an informative report, and has an important symbolic potential within the processes of political legitimation at local level.

Another reticular initiative relevant to the affirmation of the ZW vision in Italy is that of the Association of Virtuous Municipalities. The network was established in 2005 on the initiative of four municipalities belonging to different territories, Monsano, in the Marche, Colorno, Emilia, Vezzano Ligure, and Liguria and Melpignano in Salento. Today, there are more than 100 municipalities adhering to the network, and urban realities such as Parma and Trento have been added. However, the objective is still to strengthen the exchange of knowledge between local administrations, especially those of small or medium size, on issues related to local development and sustainability. One of the most relevant issues is precisely that of waste management, where inland areas, small towns, and rural areas can present innovative solutions with a low environmental impact compared to those of metropolitan cities, even though lack of financial resources and administrative expertise often does not allow local communities to genuinely govern their territories.

3

THE OWNERSHIP AND GOVERNANCE MODELS OF URBAN WASTE SERVICES[1]

ABSTRACT

Chapter 3 discusses existing management models and corporate governance best practices for waste management firms. It provides some relevant experiences across Europe. It offers a focus on the ongoing remunicipalization process in the public service provision and urban waste management.

Keywords: Management models; public ownership; consortia; remunicipalization; privatization; corporate governance

3.1 THE ROLE OF OWNERSHIP AND POTENTIAL IMPACTS OF DIFFERENT MANAGEMENT MODELS

The provision of urban waste services is organized based on different strategic choices. Urban waste management activities could be managed in an integrated way by waste operators that provide all the urban waste services, from collection to treatment and disposal. However, there are also cases where some of the activities included in the urban waste management value chain are provided by several different operators. In these cases, there could be competition among them. Indeed, urban waste operators could compete to get customers (e.g., with an open competition for domestic waste collection) or to obtain public contracts through competitive tendering procedures to manage the urban waste service in municipalities. In these latter cases, Directive 2014/24/EU on public procurement and 2014/23/EU on concession contracts apply (BiPRO/CRI, 2015).

1 This chapter was written by Giulia Romano.

Generally, municipalities throughout Europe can decide whether to deliver waste management services directly, alone or with other municipalities, or to delegate the waste services to independent firms (public, mixed, or private) (Soukopová & Vaceková, 2018). This free choice is a consequence of a contingency approach (Donaldson, 2001) followed by the European Union (EU) framework that allows freedom of organization. With this approach, national and local authorities can take into account both structure and environmental contingencies and define the most suited management model for urban waste service provision. Thus, from an ownership point of view, urban waste operators could be publicly owned, mixed owned, or privately owned, and could operate directly or indirectly, through a delegated management model.

In fact, as for other public services, different management models coexist in the urban waste management industry, ranging from direct provision by municipalities to totally privatized models with involvement of private investor-owned firms (Fig. 3.1).

As suggested by Tavares, *the typical municipal bureau operates under administrative law, is tax-financed and subject to competitive budget allocations and is entirely dependent upon the preferences of local elected officials* (Tavares, 2017, p. 698; Tavares & Camões, 2010).

For example, in the Austrian capital city, Vienna, the Municipal Department 48 ("Abfallwirtschaft, Straßenreinigung und Fuhrpark – MA 48") is responsible for the waste management, street cleaning, and vehicle fleet, and is part of the environmental division of the city of Vienna administration. Similarly, the Helsinki Region Environmental Services Authority (HSY) in Finland is a municipal body that produces waste management and water services and provides information on the Helsinki Metropolitan Area and environment. HSY collects the municipal solid waste (household and public service sector mixed waste and biowaste) and completes the collection of waste under extended producer responsibility, such as the collection of packaging

	Public	Private
Direct management	Municipalities	Privately owned firms Coops or other community-owned supplies
Delegated management	Publicly owned utilities	Privately owned firms
	Mixed owned utilities	

Fig. 3.1. Management Models in Public Service Provision.

from households and waste of electrical and electronic equipment (WEEE-waste) at sorting stations.

Along with the direct service provision by the municipalities using their own plants, equipment, and employees, many municipalities create cooperation models through consortia or associations of municipalities that share duties and costs, considering the economies of scale and aiming to apply best practices in broader contexts (Bel & Gradus, 2018). For example, LIPOR in Porto is the Intermunicipal Waste Management entity created in 1982 and includes eight municipalities that are responsible for the management, valorization, and treatment of municipal solid waste produced in Greater Porto (Box 3.1).

Greater Porto is an area with approximately 972,000 inhabitants, producing about 520,000 tons of municipal solid waste per year. While municipalities directly operate waste collection activities, LIPOR supports them to find the best ways to realize effective separate waste collection and is directly responsible of waste treatment activities, also extending and building new treatment infrastructures and extending the existing ones. Within its competencies, LIPOR also cooperates and supports municipalities in raising environmental awareness, communication, and training.

As highlighted by Bel and Gradus (2018) and Soukopová and Vaceková (2018), intermunicipal cooperation increased its importance in recent years, although the number of studies investigating this issue remains small (Bel & Gradus, 2018). Meta-analysis of existing studies about intermunicipal cooperation highlighted that there could be several factors encouraging cooperation among municipalities, including fiscal restrictions, professional management, environmental factors, local income, and economies of scale (Bel & Warner, 2016).

Expected financial savings can be a strong motivation to cooperate, even if the real effect is still unclear, as highlighted by conflicting results about the impact of intermunicipal cooperation on waste management costs (Soukopová & Vaceková, 2018). This indicates the influential role of internal aspects of cooperation, such as the ownership share of an intermunicipal waste collection company, the presence of an institutional arrangement, the participation of municipal representatives in the boards of a waste utility, or the presence of independent board members or managers of the intermunicipal waste utility, profit generation, and duration of service (Soukopová & Vaceková, 2018).

Box 3.1

The Corporate Governance Experience of LIPOR in Portugal.

LIPOR – Intermunicipal Waste Management of Greater Porto – has, since its inception, maintained the legal status of a Municipality Association and was established in 1982 as an Association on November 12th of the same year. Currently, LIPOR has eight associated municipalities: Espinho, Gondomar, Maia, Matosinhos, Porto, Póvoa de Varzim, Valongo, and Vila do Conde. Although it started with five municipalities, in May 1985, the cities of Matosinhos and Vila do Conde were admitted as members. Subsequently, in February 1999, the Municipality of Póvoa de Varzim was also admitted as an associate.

Over time, the legislation governing the Association of Municipalities has changed in order to enhance synergies and promote economies of scale, as part of the powers granted to it by law. Thus, Municipality Associations are currently a typical case of the so-called public associations – one of the ways to apply the principles of the elimination of bureaucracy in public administration and to bring services closer to the people, as set out in Article 267(1) of the Portuguese Constitution, as revised in 1982.

Currently, LIPOR, as an Association of Municipalities, should comply the regulation which establishes the legal framework for local government, approves the status of Intermunicipal Entities, defines the legal system for the transfer of powers from the State to Local Authorities and Intermunicipal Entities, and approves the legal system of Municipal Associations.

In respect of the Portuguese legal framework, Associations of Municipalities shall be governed by the rules applicable to legal persons under public law and shall be subject to the "State's legal system for financial and property administration."

According to the Statutes, the governing bodies of LIPOR are the Intermunicipal Assembly and the Board of Directors. The Intermunicipal Assembly is the deliberative body of LIPOR and is composed of the Chairman and two Councilors from each of the Associated Municipalities, comprising a total of 24 members. Among its main attributions, should highlight the approval of the Budget, Business Plans and of the Report, Balance Sheet, and Accounts of the Association.

The Board of Directors is the executive body, composed of five effective directors and three alternate directors, which represent the Associated Municipalities and are elected by the Intermunicipal Assembly from among its members. All of the eight members regularly take part in the meetings and in the decisions of the organization, which are usually decided by unanimity. The Board of Directors has regular weekly/biweekly meetings, which shows a strong commitment with the Association.

The independence of the members of the governing bodies (Intermunicipal Assembly and Board of Directors) is assured by the process of scrutiny of Municipal Elections. In fact, these positions are highly political, as elected Mayors are automatically assigned to LIPOR's Intermunicipal Assembly. As for the remaining members, they are assigned by the Municipality, from among the elected Councilors. The Intermunicipal Assembly appoints the Chief Executive Officer (CEO) proposed by the Board of Directors, who shall be in charge of the professional executive management of the Association, with the assistance of the heads of the different units, who are part of the senior management of the organization.

The verification of incompatibilities and impediments contribute to ensuring impartiality when performing public service and is regulated by law. The members of the Intermunicipal Assembly and Board of Directors receive no remuneration, given that, by law, they are already paid by the respective municipalities (to guarantee transparency and exemption).

Being a public entity with high political visibility (eg. the Municipality of Porto is the second biggest city in Portugal) and following its Social Responsibility Policy, LIPOR voluntarily outlined a set of principles that ensure an integrity system, preventing corruption cases. Among the measures implemented to promote ethics and inhibit corruption, LIPOR adopted the Ethics Code, LIPOR's Board of Directors has approved the "Corruption Risk and Related Offences Management Plan," as a support mechanism for the management of anticorruption measures, which is in accordance with the guidelines set by the Portuguese Corruption Prevention Council. Four areas were identified as being more susceptible to corruption or related offenses: Public Procurement, Granting of Benefits, Human Resources, and Financial Management.

Source: *LIPOR*.

In the urban waste industry, there are also waste utilities totally or partly owned (through the so-called mixed ownership model) by public owners (mainly municipalities or the State) and/or by private owners, and some of them are listed companies.

In urban waste management, municipal waste utilities are corporations, i.e., independent firms. Specifically, they *are single-purpose organizations not allowed to levy taxes, rely on revenues derived from user fees, are governed by an appointed, rather than elected, executive board, and have independent corporate status* (Tavares & Camões, 2010, p. 535). These utilities are hybrid organizations as they are political organizations and enterprises at the same time. Policymakers *trade off bureaucratic costs of in-house production with agency costs of external delegation to municipal corporations when deciding the governance structure to deliver local public services* (Tavares & Camões, 2010, p. 587). Indeed, municipally owned enterprises (MOEs) have a vaster legal and managerial autonomy than that of in-house operators, owing to their legal status that allows regulation by public or private commercial law instead of constraints in force for municipal departments.

There are several drivers that lead to the adoption of municipal corporations and concern, among others, service features, institutional and regulatory frameworks, and financial constraints (Tavares, 2017). In general, Tavares (2017) highlighted that the municipal corporation model is applied mainly for the provision of utilities such as in waste collection and treatment, as it better fits the scale required, and it provides more elasticity in managing personnel, procurement, and financial procedures. Previous literature highlighted that MOEs are being increasingly used to provide local public services; however, owing to the scarcity of literature on this topic, the efficiency and effectiveness of service provision is till debatable, encouraging additional research (Voorn, Van Genugten, & van Thiel, 2017). Voorn et al. (2017) showed that MOEs are frequently more efficient than local administrations in refuse collection; thus, they are a feasible means for providing some local public services if municipalities have the needed capacity of starting and handling complex contracts. In contrast, regarding the Tuscan context in Italy, Romano, Ferreira, Marques, and Carosi (2020) highlighted that public management models (direct or delegated) have similar efficiency results than those of mixed or privately owned firms and that direct public provision is more efficient than delegated management. Therefore, they conclude that privatization does not seem to exert significant improvement in performance results and also that direct management could be beneficial.

On this matter, Simões and Marques (2012) claimed that the public provision of waste services might yield better efficiency than the private provision in the richest areas.

In contrast, some challenges have been highlighted regarding corporate governance problems in MOEs. Indeed, the presence of politicians as members of the shareholders' meeting and as board members of MOEs could raise agency costs and moral hazard problems. Bergh, Erlingsson, Gustafsson, and Wittberg (2019) highlighted that *owner-representation in MOE boards emanates from what amounts to a third-order delegation-problem (i.e., from voter to party, party to council/municipal board, council/municipal board to MOE boards). Therefore, owners that are represented on boards of a publicly owned corporation are substantially different compared to owners' representation in private enterprises. Local politicians are agents which may have a personal interest and agendas that may or may not be at odds with the interests of the electorate* (Bergh et al., 2019, p. 326). Thus, the authors highlighted the lack of transparency in the process of appointment of board members as well as a lack of competencies required that could lead to corruption practices (Bergh et al., 2019). Indeed, Menozzi, Gutierrez Urtiaga, and Vannoni (2011) highlighted that politically connected directors are the majority of boards of directors in

Italian public utilities and exercise a positive and significant effect on employment but a negative effect on economic results.

Examples of provision of urban waste services by municipally owned utilities could be found in Germany, e.g., the capital city, Berlin operates Berliner Stadtreinigungsbetriebe (BSR), a municipally owned company, which is one of the most relevant urban waste operators in Europe.

While BSR is directly owned by a local government entity, there are other examples of indirect control from municipalities: Ljubljana in Slovenia, where the publicly owned firm Voka Snaga operates. The owner of Voka Snaga is Javni Holding Ljubljana d.o.o., whose shares are held by seven Slovenian municipalities.

Other examples are Contarina in Veneto Region in the northeast of Italy, which provides the public service to 49 municipalities that, through the Priula Consortium, owned its shares, and ASCIT in Tuscany (Box 3.2).

Box 3.2

A Small-sized Public-owned Firm: ASCIT SpA in Capannori Municipality.

ASCIT SpA was founded in 1997 as a Special Consortium Company by some municipalities in Lucca province. Subsequently, it was transformed into a joint stock company in 2004, and some municipalities left the company as shareholders.

The six municipalities served by ASCIT as urban waste management operator were ASCIT's direct owners until the end of 2015. The Capannori Municipality held over 49% of the company's capital, being the most relevant shareholder. In 2015, the six shareholder municipalities signed the dedicated capital increase of Retiambiente SpA, conferring their entire stake in the company ASCIT. Currently, ASCIT is a completely public company subject to the direction and coordination of the sole shareholder Retiambiente SpA.

Retiambiente is a fully publicly owned company that acquired control of some of the companies that dealt with the management of solid urban waste in Tuscany at the end of 2015: ERSU (Versilia), ASCIT (Lucca plain), GEOFOR (Pisa), and ESA (Island of Elba). In 2016, Retiambiente acquired REA (Rosignano), and then, in 2017, SEA AMBIENTE (Viareggio and Camaiore).

Currently, Retiambiente has 99 Tuscan municipalities as shareholders. The municipality of Capannori holds 3.69% of the capital. The four partners with the highest share of capital are the Municipalities of Pisa, Viareggio, Pontedera and Rosignano, with 20.28%, 13.59%, 13.12%, and 12, 36%, respectively, having over 59% of the capital together.

The project linked to the creation of Retiambiente allowed the creation of a company with total public capital by the municipalities belonging to one of the optimal territorial areas (ATO) of Tuscany (in particular, the Toscana Costa, ATO).

After the creation of Retiambiente, the original plan included a subsequent capital increase to be signed by a private partner, selected by a public tender. However, on January 9, 2017, the public tender for the choice of the private/industrial partner to be assigned at least 45% of Retiambiente's share capital was canceled. Subsequently, with resolution no. 14 of December 19, 2018, ATO laid the foundations for the abandonment of the mixed company management model in favor of the in-house model, maintaining Retiambiente as a completely publicly owned company to guarantee a direct control over both the parent company and the operating companies such as ASCIT.

As far as the corporate governance model, ASCIT adopted two-tier model until 2017, with the presence of a management board and a supervisory board. From February 9, 2017, the company adjusted its bylaws to the new rules contained in Legislative Decree 175/2016 (consolidated law on public companies) and has moved from the dual management and control system to the traditional system, characterized by a board of directors and a board of auditors.

The ASCIT board of directors consists of three members, two men and a woman. The Chairman Giuseppe Gatti also holds the position of director of Retiambiente.

Starting in 2010, the company identified Dr. Roger Bizzarri as General Manager. The general manager was selected by a personnel research company with the aim of evaluating potential candidates preferably "external" to the area served to avoid mingling and potential reciprocal conditioning. The selection was transparent and independent, in contrast with what frequently occurred in the context of publicly owned companies.

Therefore, the president and general manager have held the position for about a decade, offering the company strategic and managerial continuity, and the collaboration shows to be successful. Both managers are graduates in business administration and have a common knowledge base, which allows them to "speak the same language." For both, it was the first experience in managing a company in the field of urban waste management, an aspect that has stimulated both to interact and confront each other, and also to introduce innovations modifying the administrative and management structure.

The board of directors, with the active support of the general manager, deals with the strategic functions, control activities, and management of the relationships with the main stakeholders.

The relationship created between chairman and general manager in ASCIT provides for continuous collaboration and exchange of information. However, the roles are quite distinct; the care of relations with the shareholders (which are, directly or indirectly, the municipalities and, therefore, the various auditors) and the comparison with their requests is a prerogative of the president. Meanwhile, the actual management as well as administrative and management decisions are entrusted to the general manager. In a company like ASCIT, with total public control, there is a high risk that the search for political consensus clashes with the improvement objectives that are identified by the administrators and managers regarding business efficiency, safeguarding of company assets, and achieving and maintaining a good rating toward banks and lenders. Therefore, the management of relations with key political interlocutors is a complex activity of confrontation and mediation, aimed at satisfying citizens' requests without diverting attention from the need to maintain the company along a path of sustainable and evolutionary development.

ASCIT started distributing dividends in 2016, providing a constant trend in recent years, which, however, led to an increase in the payout ratio because of the decrease in profits in the last two years.

A further available management model is the mixed ownership one, also called institutionalized public–private partnership. In these utilities, public and private shareholders hold part of the share capital, and the private shareholder is usually selected through a public tender procedure (Bognetti & Robotti, 2007). The majority could be held either by the public or the private shareholders (Bognetti & Robotti, 2007).

Cruz and Marques (2012) highlighted that this model, where public owners and private investors coexist as shareholders present *the biggest challenges for public authorities who decide to embrace this type of agreement* (Cruz & Marques, 2012). Indeed, the authors found that mixed companies could be created to circumvent budgetary constraints with direct undesirable consequences for citizens using public services. Further, this model entails several "traps" that could constrain the expected favorable effects to the public interest. Although mixed-owned utilities are created to realize an equilibrium between social and efficiency goals, the private sector's objectives usually prevail at the expenses of protecting the public general interest. The authors conclude that "no man can serve two masters," (Laffont & Tirole, 1991) and in this case, private aims prevail (Cruz & Marques, 2012).

Corporate governance rules are critical. Even when the public owners held the majority of shares as shareholders, the presence of private owners could present some challenges, i.e., the public shareholders usually must renounce to the possibility of appointing the CEO and/or the majority of board members and give broad powers to the private partners to define strategies and how to share the efficiency gains among stakeholders (McDonald, 2018). Thus, there is sometimes a lack of control power in public shareholders' hands, with public owners that should accept private-driven decisions, including the dividend policy (Romano & Guerrini, 2019) and the service quality levels allowed by regulatory schemes (Valdovinos, 2012). Particularly, in public service provision, the *extreme complexity involved in the whole life-cycle management of these companies usually leads to a poor protection of the public interest* (Cruz & Marques, 2012, p. 737).

Literature has also highlighted that mixed enterprises have been created by municipalities to exploit economies of scale and scope, without necessarily renouncing to loose leadership and direction of the entrusted utility (Bognetti & Robotti, 2007). Further, multibusiness strategies in mixed enterprises are proportionally higher than those in other management models (Bognetti & Robotti, 2007).

The public–private conflict could be particularly relevant in case of listed companies, where stock markets, investors, and analysts have a relevant role in the managerial decision-making process. In this sense, the risk to underestimate the potential conflict between public interest to be achieved by public service operators and the profit-seeking behavior of private partners is high (Hall, 2001).

Examples of listed mixed-owned waste utilities could be found in Italy, where big multiutility firms (A2A, Acea, Hera, and Iren groups) provide several different public services, from waste management to water services, from electricity to gas distribution, and are listed on the Italian stock exchange. They are among the most relevant listed firms in terms of capitalization.[2]

They have thousands of shareholders, with different contrasting goals, from small individual shareholders to big international investors, from sovereign funds to municipalities, which hold the majority of shares.

Recently, the Italian corporate governance code for listed companies changed (Comitato Corporate Governance, 2020); it highlighted the need for directors of listed companies to adopt strategies oriented toward the sustainability of their business. In contrast to those in the past, the code underlined the main goal of creating long-term value for the benefit of shareholders while considering the interests of the stakeholders relevant to its activity.

2 A2A has as relevant shareholders the municipalities of Milan and Brescia, both with 25% of share capital. The two public owners have a shareholders' agreement to jointly define the corporate governance rules. Acea, which manages some urban waste treatment plants, has the Municipality of Roma as the majority shareholder, with 51% of share capital. Relevant private owners are Suez SA, a multinational utility firm, and a private entrepreneur, leader of a leading Italian construction group.Hera has 46.6% of its share capital in public owners' hands, i.e., municipalities located in different regions of Italy, from Emilia-Romagna to Veneto to Friuli Venezia Giulia. However, municipalities have more than 61% of vote rights, and they stipulated a shareholders' agreement to define corporate governance rules. Similarly, Iren has the municipalities from Liguria, Piedmont, and Emilia-Romagna Regions as majority shareholders. Thus, shareholders' agreements and the bylaws give the majority of voting rights on some relevant firm decisions to municipalities. *Source:* Consob website.

Finally, the private management model could be implemented that involves complete privatization of waste management activities with the entrustment of a fully private firm, needing very strong regulations to avoid monopolistic rents. Further, along with corruption in public tendering activities, there is also high risk of not being able to improve efficiency after privatization because *in principle there is no magic line that separates firms from politicians once they are privatized* (Schleifer & Vishny, 1994, p. 998).

The waste industry throughout Europe has assumed different characteristics in terms of management models adopted. For example, looking for experiences in the capital cities of the 28 EU countries (European Commission, 2015), the majority have a public management model.

Some European capital cities have direct public management, such as in Wien (Austria), with the Abfallwirtschaft, Straßenreinigung und Fuhrpark (MA 48). Others have a delegated public management such as in Berlin (BSR, Berliner Stadtreinigungsbetriebe), Ljubljana (Voka Snaga), and Rome (AMA SpA). In Brussels, the Brussels-Capital Region has established a number of regional bodies, i.e., institutions of public benefit and nonprofit organizations, to provide public services to citizens. Bruxelles-Propreté, in particular, is accountable for environmental preservation (preserving the public space clean and in order), waste collection and management in the Brussels-Capital Region, and employs about 2,400 people. From a legal point of view, Bruxelles-Propreté is a type A pararegional entity acting under the authority of the Minister of the Government of the Region of Brussels-Capital in charge of Climate Transition, Environment, Energy, and Participatory Democracy.

Other capital cities have a private system such as in Dublin, where citizens can choose a private operator for waste collection on the basis of charges and services provided.

In several European countries such as Italy, Slovenia, and Portugal, there is a consortium system in force for managing packaging waste under producer responsibility schemes (Box 3.3).

It is interesting to note that most European capitals have decided to retain the management of the urban waste management service in public hands, highlighting the relevance that policymakers deserve in direct and delegated public management models in the most relevant cities of each country. Indeed, capital cities are usually the political and touristic focus of countries, and, usually, a relevant part of the national population lives in them. A direct control over the management of one of the most relevant public services is of utmost importance, which could explain the choice of most capital cities throughout EU.

Box 3.3

National Packaging Consortium in Italy (Retrieved from: http://www.conai.org/en/)

"CONAI, the National Packaging Consortium, is a private nonprofit consortium. It is a system forming the response from private companies to a problem of collective interest, i.e., the environment, in accordance with the guidelines and objectives set by the political system. To date, 800,000 companies producing or using packaging have joined the consortium system.

Founded on the basis of the Ronchi Decree of 1997, the consortium marked the transition from a management system based on landfills to an integrated system based on the prevention, recovery, and recycling of six packaging materials: steel, aluminum, paper, wood, plastic, and glass.

CONAI collaborates with municipalities according to specific agreements governed by the ANCI-CONAI National Framework Agreement and serves as a guarantee to citizens that any materials from separate waste collections are fully used through proper recovery and recycling processes.

All companies that join the consortium pay a compulsory contribution that serves as a form of financing, allowing CONAI to support separate waste collection and packaging waste recycling.

CONAI directs the activities and guarantees the recovery results of six consortia: steel (Ricrea), aluminum (Cial), paper/cardboard (Comieco), wood (Rilegno), plastic (Corepla), and glass (Coreve), ensuring the necessary links between these consortia and public administration."

Homsy (2016) highlighted the relevant role that municipal utilities may play in sustainability, policymaking, and implementation, and affirmed that the presence of local utilities sustains sustainability action in local communities owing to their capacity, both fiscal and technical.

3.2 BOARD OF DIRECTORS AND OTHER CORPORATE GOVERNANCE RULES

Along with a focus on the ownership of urban waste operators, it is important to analyze the broad corporate governance of a utility, i.e., analyzing the characteristics and roles of owners, board of directors, and management team. Indeed, to evaluate the corporate governance rules in force in a firm, it is essential to know who has the power to appoint members of the board of directors and of the management team in force, and then, to explore how these members and managers are selected and how the powers and responsibilities are distributed among them.

Publicly owned firms are increasingly important. As highlighted in an Organisation for Economic Co-operation and Development (OECD) report, 14% of global stock market capitalization is owned by the public sector (De La Cruz, Medina, & Tang, 2019). Thus, since 2005, OECD has drafted some guidelines for the corporate governance of state-owned enterprises (SOEs) to provide an international benchmark for public owners to exercise their functions.

The version in force was drafted in 2015 (OECD, 2015) and aimed at giving *concrete advice to countries on how to manage more effectively their responsibilities as company owners, thus helping to make state-owned enterprises more competitive, efficient and transparent.*

In several countries, some relevant changes occurred in the implementation of the SOE Guidelines in the period 2013–2018 (OECD, 2020), such as those in corporate governance reporting rules and professionalization of board members. A special OECD report on national practices applied to Boards of Directors of SOEs highlighted the efforts to professionalize boards, ensure independence, and avoid undue political intervention, although more efforts are still required (OECD, 2013) (Box 3.4).

Box 3.4

Board of Director Good Practices in Organisation for Economic Co-operation and Development (OECD) Countries.

Summary of Good Practices

Role of Boards of Directors

- The board plays a central function in state-owned enterprise (SOE) governance and should act as an intermediary between the ownership function and the SOE's executive management.
- The role of the board should be clearly defined and founded in legislation, preferably according to general company law.

- The role of the board of directors should focus on strategic guidance and corporate performance, and shift focus away from a traditional "conformance" role.
- The state should inform the board of its objectives and priorities through proper channels to ensure the board maximum autonomy and independence.

Nomination Framework and Practices

- A robust nomination framework is one that clearly specifies the nominating power is transparent and is consistent in its application.
- Ministerial or executive powers normally have the ultimate responsibility for nominations. This brings legitimacy to the process, but it should not undermine the role of the ownership function.
- Where feasible, board appointments should be subject to coordination or consensus on a whole-of-government basis.
- Board appointments, even in wholly owned SOEs, should be entrusted to the annual general meeting of shareholders.
- Establishing a transparent and consistent method to identify applicants from a wider pool of talent will improve board composition and bring uniformity in the assessment process.
- Specialized bodies in charge of advising or accrediting the nominations can bring further objectivity and transparency to the nomination process.
- The Board should be involved in the nomination process in an advisory capacity.
- Mechanisms should exist to facilitate nongovernment shareholders' participation in the board nomination process.

Board Composition

- Persons directly linked with the executive powers should not sit on SOE boards. Other state representatives should be nominated based on qualifications, subject to specific vetting mechanisms.

- Independent directors should be independent from management, government, and business relationships. Specific safeguards should be established to verify that nominees comply with requirements.
- Employee representatives can enrich board discussion; the appointment process should ensure that such persons are qualified, as well as representative of the SOE's staff.
- Certain eligibility requirements may be needed, but good practice increasingly relies on tailored approaches to identify the right mix between skills, experience, and personal characteristics.
- For all other than direct ownership representatives, relevant commercial or financial expertise is viewed as essential qualifications.
- Reasonable limits on maximum number of board appointments are important to ensure that directors have sufficient time to carry out their duties.
- Diversity preferences may add value to boards, but should not rise to the level where the ability to attract candidates with the right skills and capabilities is imperiled.
- Restricting board membership to nationals should be limited to cases where there is a demonstrated need for such rules, considering that it can act as a barrier to attract the right talent.

Training and Induction

- Induction programs should match the needs of each board. They should serve as a way to improve effectiveness of board members.
- General training for boards of directors should not be a formal requirement; however, ongoing professional development should be encouraged and supported.

Remuneration

- Board remuneration should reflect the market conditions to the extent that this is necessary to attract and retain highly qualified directors.
- Remuneration policies of civil servants serving on SOE boards should be carefully considered to ensure the right incentives.

Boardroom Efficiency

- The key to the board efficiency is a Chair who can build an effective team by exercising leadership, diplomacy, and a deep understanding of the business.
- Specialized committees can contribute to the efficiency of the board but should not detract from the responsibility of the full board.
- Board committees should be made up of independent and technically literate board members to ensure efficiency.

Source: *OECD (2013).*

The peculiarities of utilities (and of waste utilities in particular) include that, in most cases, they have municipalities or other local public bodies as owners. However, guidelines stated for SOE could be applied with adaptations to municipality-owned utilities in most cases and could serve as recommendations for local owners and policymakers at local level.

The presence of local politicians among decision-makers and the local spectrum of activities make the corporate governance of such firms peculiar, limiting transparency and citizen oversight to a local audience. Therefore, it is important to understand if best practices are applied, looking to principles and suggestions following the same approach applied for listed companies through well-known corporate governance codes. However, diverse approaches are followed in different countries.

Research investigating corporate governance issues in public utilities is quite scarce. It has been highlighted that the close connection between utilities and local governments in Italy determines the prevalence of politically connected directors on the boards of Italian utilities (Romano & Guerrini, 2014), exerting negative effect on the utilities' performance (Menozzi et al., 2011).

However, regarding water utilities, high efficiency levels were found in utilities with substantial presence of politically connected directors (more than two-thirds of board members being politically connected) and by firms with more than six board members (Romano, Salvati, & Guerrini, 2018).

Other empirical studies found that the boards of Italian water utilities are controlled by politically connected directors, who support access to debt. The study also showed that board size and composition, in terms of the age and educational background of members, influence economic and financial performance (Romano & Guerrini, 2014) and efficiency (Romano et al., 2018).

Soft laws are applied in some cases. For example, DANVA, the Danish Water and Wastewater Association in Denmark, defined some principles for good corporate governance in utilities held by municipalities (DANVA, 2017). These principles are included in soft law, so they can be applied on the basis of the voluntary comply-or-explain principle and adapted to different contexts and situations (Box 3.5).

In other contexts, corporate governance rules for publicly owned firms are defined with law, and thus, they are compulsory and must be applied. For example, in Italy, corporate governance of firms with public owners is regulated by a law (Consolidated Act on Public Participated Companies, Legislative Decree no. 175 issued on August 2016) that defines rules for board size and board members remuneration.[3] Further, it defines the rules that apply for board members' selection, avoiding appointment of members with conflicts of interest, involved in maladministration or that had previous appointments as politicians.

This law was enacted to limit the State owner's involvement in commercial activities of SOEs, preventing public administration from establishing new SOEs whose purpose is to produce goods and services not strictly necessary for the pursuit of their shareholders' institutional mandate.

Further, the Legislative Decree 33/2013 requires Italian Public Administration to provide information about every member of the board of directors/auditors to their participated enterprises, with special focus on the economic remunerations agreed. Information should also be reported on dedicated sections of the SOE websites, as well as to the public ownership entities.

Following recognized best practices, specific relevance should be devoted to the selection of best board members through transparent and broadly framed recruitment processes based on clear eligibility rules and transparent

---

3 The Legislative Decree 175/2016 provides that the maximum yearly compensation for any manager/worker of state-owned enterprises (SOEs) cannot exceed 240,000 euros (listed companies and those with listed financial instruments issued are excluded). The above-mentioned law also states that the Minister of the Economy and Finance will formulate a ministerial decree to define further lower compensation, which will eventually be applied to the SOEs.Until the above mentioned decree is issued, to determine compensation of executive directors, the Ministerial Decree 166/2013 still applies with a classification of SOEs into 3 groups, determined on the basis of relevant indicators derived from the official financial statements, i.e., value of production, investments, and number of employees.Further requirements for the candidates to the boards of directors/auditors of SOEs are included in two specific acts, both issued by the Minister of the Economy and Finance in June 2013.

Box 3.5

Danish Principles of Good Governance for Utilities Owned by Municipalities.

The DANVA principles for good corporate governance are divided into six parts:

(1) Framework for exercising ownership

(2) Active exercise of rights of ownership in the utilities

(3) Interplay between companies and owner municipalities

(4) Structure of the Board of Directors

(5) Interplay between the Board of Directors and the Management Team

(6) Other matters

The broader corporate governance lies on the following division of responsibilities among the main corporate governance actors.

Division of Responsibilities

Owner Municipality

- Shall ensure that there is a composition of the membership of Board of Directors that is appropriate in relation to the business activities and particular circumstances of the company which also pays due regard to the Articles of Association.
- Has an obligation to maintain an overall supervision and to express views concerning developments within the company.
- Has an obligation to act should the developments within the company so dictate.
- Shall consider the overall strategic framework for the company.

The Board of Directors

- Has the overall responsibility for decisions regarding operations and investments.

- Shall exercise strategic management, i.e. actively participate in the preparation of the company's overall strategy and goals and reach decisions concerning matters that extend beyond daily operations.
- Is responsible for being a sparring partner for and to attend to the supervision of the Management Team.
- Has an obligation to support the general supervision conducted by the municipality and actively exercise ownership in order to ensure, inter alia, that the owner municipality receives the relevant information.

Management Team

- Has the responsibility for the overall general management of the company.
- Has an obligation to support the strategic management of the Board of Directors by continually and at an appropriate level providing information on circumstances in the company and include the Board of Directors in decisions of an unusual nature or of great importance for the company.

Source: DANVA (2017).

Among others, the DANVA's principles require that *the municipality or municipalities draw up an ownership document that summarizes their views on the rationale, objectives and overall strategic framework of ownership*. This ownership document should be made publicly available.

Regarding the Board of Directors size and composition, *it is recommended that the Board of the Utility companies consist of an operational size, often with 6–11 members*. Further, *where the Board of Directors needs additional members based on particular expertise, two additional members should be recruited as a minimum*, and *the Board of Directors strives for a balanced composition of men and women, and as a means of achieving this establishes targets for the gender distribution*.

Board remuneration should be clear, and a remuneration policy is suggested. In addition, *it is recommended that clear information is provided on any "dependencies" that each board member has, and that the information is made available to the general public on the company's website, for example*.

With reference to the interaction between the Board of Directors and the Management Team, DANVA's principles recommend that *at least once a year the Board of Directors evaluates the work and results of the Management Team in accordance with preestablished criteria*.

Interestingly, the principles recommended that relevant policies for social responsibility should be defined in accordance with the owner strategy. Further, at least once a year, an account of the work with social responsibility should be defined. Finally, *it is recommended that the Board of Directors considers whether a whistleblower scheme should be established within the company to provide the opportunity for the appropriate and confidential reporting of any serious misconduct or suspicions in this regard.*

remuneration, which can attract professional and authoritative members as board members and management team leaders. Eligibility rules should encompass independence, professionalism, competence, and honorability as guidelines for the selection of board members.

Principles enforcing board diversity in terms of gender, professionalism, and age should be defined along with independence and honorability rules. The sole independence, honorability, or professionalism focus in guidelines for selection of utilities' board membership is insufficient and ineffective, as these characteristics should be concurrently be requested to board members.

Looking for the best human capital to manage operators involved in public services is of utmost importance to devote the needed attention and efforts to improve efficiency, quality of service, and social and environmental sustainability.

3.3 THE REMUNICIPALIZATION PROCESS IN PUBLIC SERVICE PROVISION AND URBAN WASTE MANAGEMENT

In past decades, some European countries have experienced a privatization wave in public service provision, and the outcomes are mixed, as desired results have not always been reached (Bel & Gradus, 2018; Petersen, Hjelmar, & Vrangbæk, 2018). Therefore, an opposite trend of remunicipalization is emerging (Becker, Beveridge, & Naumann, 2015; Clifton, Warner, Gradus, & Bel, 2019; Hall & Nguyen, 2012; Kishimoto, Lobina, & Petitjean, 2015), with an increasing request to directly manage the public services coming from citizens and policymakers, mainly through totally publicly owned firms with a direct delegation of activities.

In Italy, the debate was stronger than that in other countries, owing to the effect of the 2011 referendum that called for terminating the remuneration of capital invested in the water management and revoking the mandatory presence of private shareholders in water utilities (even more, in general, in public utilities) (Landriani, Lepore, D'Amore, Pozzoli, & Alvino, 2019).

Germany is also experiencing a remunicipalization trend *to achieve higher environmental standards, better labor conditions, fairer pricing and even greater urban democracy* (Becker et al., 2015, p. 76). Similarly, the remunicipalization process followed by the municipality of Paris in water service provision is well-known (Valdovinos, 2012).

There are plenty reasons for the remunicipalization trend in public service provision. Clifton et al. (2019) recently highlighted that *remunicipalization is as an important trend in public service delivery* even if *the term is used in different, and sometimes, contradictory, ways, leading to conceptual confusion, in turn, affecting attempts to quantify this development* (Clifton et al., 2019, p. 1 and 3).

Clifton et al. (2019) distinguished the drivers of remunicipalization into pragmatic reasons and political and transformative processes. Among the former, increasing the service quality, circumventing oligopolies, caring of workers' conditions, improving efficiency, eliminating tendering and monitoring costs, and lowering capital cost are the most frequent goals pursued by policymakers (Hall, 2012; Hall & Nguyen, 2012).

Regarding political and transformative processes, remunicipalization is intended as a different, more democratic, form of public service provision, including more social and environmental justice. As highlighted by the authors, both political transformation and pragmatic process of contract and market management are happening nowadays (Clifton et al., 2019).

In Italy, Germany (Becker et al., 2015), and France (Valdovinos, 2012), a relevant driver of remunicipalization is the willingness to retain all the possible levers of strategy and policy about how to best manage the urban waste service in public hands. Indeed, even the partial presence in the share capital of private partners implies that the decision-making process should be shared with at least another shareholder with a different approach to performance measurement. As experienced by Contarina SpA, a remunicipalized waste utility that operates in the Treviso Province in Italy, a private partner needs dividends to justify the investment, and its strategy and business model could include incineration, in contrast with the environmental and social goals of a municipality wishing to adopt a circular economy approach.

Publicly owned waste companies do not need to generate profits, and cost reductions could be used to increase investments or to directly benefit the citizens through lower tariffs. Moreover, it has been highlighted that public ownership supports intellectual capital creation and sharing better than private ownership (Minoja & Romano, 2021). Public ownership seems more suitable to pursue sustainable performance than the private one, owing to the former's lower attention on profits and dividends, willingness to invest even when delayed returns are expected, and deeper relationships based on more trust with the community (Minoja & Romano, 2021).

As described by Corvellec, Bramryd, and Hultman (2011), municipalities should entrust waste management services through a public tender, but exceptions are possible if two conditions are met: *municipally owned companies must derive only a marginal share of their income from customers other than their municipal owners (activity criterion), and the second is that these municipal owners must exercise a degree of control over these companies that is equivalent to what it exercises over its own departments (control criterion)* (Corvellec et al., 2011, p. 517). Thus, in public service provision, rivalry is not an issue for publicly owned utilities. Indeed, in the EU, in-house delegation creates a local monopoly regime that restrict the opportunity of a utility operating outside the area of the shareholder municipalities to a small part of total revenues (in Italy, 20%). Thus, their experiences and competences can be transmitted to other companies or municipalities without any unwanted effects on rivalry (Minoja & Romano, 2021).

The absence of rivalry implies that successful publicly owned firms can share their business models and intellectual capital to other firms and municipalities. They can spread these successful experiences in other context in a more rapid and less risky way than privately owned firms. Moreover, the low pressure on profits, linked to the public ownership status, enables publicly owned waste firms to transfer their knowledge at affordable prices. In Italy, similar experiences have been realized by Contarina, with a partnership with two start-ups, one in the same Veneto Region called Valpe Ambiente and the other in another Italian Region (Emilia-Romagna) called Alea Ambiente, and by ASCIT through an intragroup collaboration with a waste utility operating in another Tuscan province (Box 3.6).

Box 3.6

Contarina SpA – A Clear Example of Resource and Knowledge Sharing from a Cutting-edge Publicly Owned Firm.

Contarina SpA is the in-house provider company operating in the Province of Treviso in the Veneto Region since 1989. It currently manages the urban waste management service in 49 municipalities for a territory of approximately 1,300 km^2 with approximately 554,000 inhabitants. The company attained in 2018 88.8% separate collection of waste with a tariff well below the national average. Their objective is to reach 96.7% separate collection by the end of 2022.

It is managed and coordinated by the publicly owned *Consiglio di Bacino Priula* (consortium) which owns 100% of the shares. The consortium oversees Contarina's activities and is in charge of tendering the service contract as well as its update, controlling activities, and providing public guarantee. The 49 Priula municipalities share the same goals, service standards, service model, and a single and homogenous tariff. This governance model avoids a fragmented decision-making process and, thus, inconsistent management.

In recent years, relevant investments have been realized to improve waste services and reach outstanding economic, environmental, and social targets: over €60,000,000 to create greater awareness and training, research and development projects for the enhancement of its structures including composting facilities, selection of recyclable waste, and conversion of its fleet of around 500 vehicles to hybrid, electric, and methane vehicles. Additionally, Contarina obtained the ISO 9001, 14001, 29990, and OHSAS 18001 certifications.

The Contarina business model is based on integrated door-to-door waste collection with a pay-as-you-throw scheme. The entire system is based on the concept of the "individual responsibility" of citizens for correctly sorting waste and the "collective responsibility" of the company in the waste collection, transport, treatment, and recovery for recycling. The waste is managed through an integrated service, which considers waste from production to treatment and recovery with a positive effect on both the environment and citizens' daily life. This model implies attention to the research and development of structures that can better contribute to material recovery and reduction of the remaining nonrecyclable dry waste, which ends up in the incinerators.

A relevant example is the creation of a unique cutting-edge plant (using the technology developed and registered by Fater SpA) for the recycling of personal absorbent products (PAP) used by all brands to obtain sterilized plastic, cellulose, and super absorbent polymers, which can then be used as valuable secondary raw materials. This technology allows the recycling of a new category of previously unsorted goods, resulting in tangible environmental advantages along with an add-on in the circular economy. Indeed, from one ton of sorted PAP waste, it is now possible to obtain up to 150, 75, and 75 kg of cellulose, plastic, and super absorbent polymer, respectively.

The core principles of Contarina's business model are a very close link with its territory and its needs, the capacity to adapt to different situations in terms of urban and social complexity, attention to innovations, and a commitment to communication, information, and citizen awareness.

What makes the Contarina model innovative is its "flexibility." Indeed, this model can be adapted and applied to any geographical, economic, social, and cultural situation, while maintaining its essential characteristics.

The door-to-door waste management model developed by Contarina has also been adopted in other territories. More specifically, in 2015, the company "applied" its model in the Belluno area thanks to the creation of the in-house provider *Valpe Ambiente*, of which it owns 19% of the shares. The *Unione Montana Agordina*, a partner of Valpe, had already attained 82% of sorted waste after only one year. In accordance with the bylaw of Valpe Ambiente, for the first nine years of activity, the General Manager of Valpe Ambiente is appointed by Contarina. Currently, the General Manager of Contarina holds this position, who was previously the CEO of Contarina. Moreover, the bylaw stated that one of the three board members could be appointed by Contarina. These two corporate governance rules allow to maintain and foster a strict link with Contarina and its business model, and give relevant levers to realize expected goals to Contarina in accordance with its values.

Similarly, owing to a collaboration agreement in 2017, the Contarina model was replicated in 13 municipalities near Forli, with the creation of the *Alea Ambiente*, a start-up in-house publicly owned company. One month after the introduction of door-to-door waste collection, the sorted waste reached 80% and the nonrecyclable dry waste 72% (the objective set was a 54% reduction). As compared to 2017, the nonrecyclable dry waste sent to incineration decreased by more than 48,000 t.

The collaboration agreement based on the principle of sharing both tangible and intangible resources (know-how, human capital, technology, etc.) fosters an industrial model that could be considered as an alternative to that of a "large" company operating in a "large" territory. Such model is based on a network of companies having a very streamlined organizational and operational structure and direct contacts with the territory served, which enables it to operate over a vast territory without losing the valuable direct link with citizens, territory, and relevant stakeholders.

Public shareholders such as municipalities could have an increasingly relevant entrepreneurial role in institutional change and in shaping environmental policies, e.g., the City of Gothenburg (Zapata & Zapata Campos, 2019). With a strong vision and policy orientation, local governments can define the management model more appropriate for their context, deciding to maintain political and strategical levers in their hands if possible, reducing the influence of other (private) shareholders in political and administrative decisions. The experience of Paris in water service remunicipalization showed how the direct involvement of local authorities is relevant, changing their role by pure political vision to active involvement in demonstrating the relevance of reasserting public control and opportunities for financial gain (Valdovinos, 2012).

In contrast, some important challenges and drawbacks are linked to public ownership. As highlighted by Corvellec et al. (2011) *municipally owned companies are ... subjected to political control. The companies operate under so-called owners' directives ... that define company objectives. Their board is composed of politically appointed members. ... A change in the political majority in municipal owners can have profound strategic implications for municipally owned ... companies. New board members can challenge the very idea that municipalities should own such a company, and can impose strategic options that have more to do with political ideology than with the operation and rationale of the company. The fact that municipalities are both owners and customers of their MSW companies determines these companies' governance* (Corvellec et al., 2011, p. 513).

The drawback highlighted by Corvellec et al. (2011) is extremely relevant, as political choices frequently affected publicly owned firm efficiency and sustainability, with excess of employees, too low tariffs, bad practices in decision-making, and even corruption and other misconducts (Romano, Masserini, & Lombardi, 2021).

Empirical studies on boards of utilities showed that politically connected directors are the majority of board members, even if the effect of their presence is still unclear (Menozzi et al., 2011; Romano et al., 2018; Romano & Guerrini, 2014).

Moreover, some public waste operators are managed at provincial or regional level, thus creating a distinction between the territory served as well as strategy and decision-making processes, with consequences on efficiency and service quality. This latter critical situation was experienced by some municipalities in the Lazio region, unsatisfied by the management practices of the urban waste management service realized by a regionally owned firm. Thus, these municipalities created Minerva Ambiente Scrl in 2019, a new firm, that was owned by a consortium of nine municipalities with a strong aim to be sustainable for the common good and future generations and to be well rooted in the territory through a governance that takes the particularities of the area served into account.

Some municipalities decided to abandon a partially privatized model (with delegation to mixed-owned companies) following the acquisition of utilities' shares from private shareholders (e.g., the Contarina case) or through the creation of publicly owned start-ups created by municipalities unsatisfied from the private management experience, in terms of service quality, economic and financial sustainability, and separate waste collection rates (Box 3.7).

Box 3.7

A Publicly Owned Start-up in Municipal Solid Waste Management: A New Path from Private to Public Management Model.

Formia Rifiuti Zero Srl. (FRZ) was created in November 2014 from the Municipality of Formia, in the south of Lazio region, Province of Latina. Formia is a highly touristic municipality, as it is located on the nice coastal area of the south Lazio, in the center of Italy.

Before the creation of the FRZ start-up, the waste management service was provided by Latina Ambiente since 2011, a mixed-owned waste utility that operated mainly in the Latina city. In fact, its shareholder capital was held by the Municipality of Latina (51%) and by a private firm (49%). Latina Ambiente failed in 2016 after a deterioration of its economic and financial data along with service quality and customer satisfaction.

FRZ was created as a company with a sole shareholder, the Formia Municipality. In December 2014, the City Council of Formia entrusted the company FRZ with the in-house provision of urban waste management service for the following eight years, renewable for a further four, with an annual budget of € 6,640,000, with the aim to activate the service from the beginning of May 2015. Since its creation, the company has a sole administrator chosen by public tender.

The company was created by the municipality, with the strong will to put Formia into the zero waste (ZW) strategy. In fact, a resolution of the Municipal Council of March 2014 defined the first steps to prepare the first FRZ Industrial Plan by following the ZW strategy.

Already in the first year of activity (2015), the positive results of separate waste collection resulted in collections from the sale of secondary raw materials that exceeded the expectations of the Industrial Plan (€ 200,000) and a reduction in the residual waste brought to landfills. The following year, the results of separate collection, in addition to fulfilling the corporate mission, have allowed revenues of € 349,899 from the sale of materials, with an increase of almost 20% compared to that in 2015 on a monthly basis. Further, the results of separate collection in 2017 allowed FRZ to cash in € 384,985.87 on the sale of materials, with an increase of over 10% compared to that in 2016.

The last available data showed a further increase of the revenues obtained from separate waste collection, reaching € 391,106 in 2018, exceeding the economic collection targets.

Important changes were introduced in the organization of the waste collection service, and above all, fundamental rules were set for the regular delivery of waste, under penalty of imposing sanctioning tools:

- Subdivision of the territory served into two areas and diversification of the collection calendar for each area;

- Activation of a citizenship awareness and information campaign to start the new service (brochures, posters, public meetings, toll-free number, etc.);
- Activation of a surveillance and control service on the correct delivery of waste by citizens;
- Absolute ban on the use of black bags for waste delivery and, therefore, the obligation to use semitransparent bags to avoid any misuse of waste bags for unsorted waste to improperly deliver recyclable waste (paper, cardboard, plastic, etc.), and allow waste collection operators to evaluate the adequacy of waste collected.

Moreover, the daily and weekly markets were regulated, for which the obligation to carry out the separate collection of waste started in July 2016, after delivery by FRZ of the needed bags and equipment.

The implementation of the new approach followed by FRZ was supported by the distribution of a kit to households; the kit consisted of disposable yellow bags for the delivery of plastic and containers for the display of waste on the defined collection days. In addition, large containers were supplied daily to commercial operators operating in the daily and weekly markets for the transfer, and then withdrawn at the end of the collection operations.

To foster the fulfillment of specific goals regarding separate waste collection rates, in 2016 and 2017, a union agreement was reached to provide a reward to employees in case of achievement of quantitative and qualitative targets. Following the achievement of these targets in 2017, a € 150 bonus was paid to each employee. In fact, FRZ reached 67% of separate waste collected in 2016, confirmed at the end of 2018. This result is much higher than the provincial and regional average (51% and 47%, respectively). Particularly good results have also been reached regarding the amount of total waste produced per capita, with significant improvements in the 2010–2018 period (-23%), also lower than the provincial and regional average (Table 3.1).

After the purchase during 2017 and 2018 of an adequate fleet of vehicles owned by FRZ to replace the more expensive rental contracts, the needs of protection and verification of these vehicles were met with modern remote control systems. The new vehicles were equipped with hardware and software devices necessary for their geolocation, tracking, and certification of the services provided, and protection of workers and vehicles, with the establishment of a Telematic Operations Center. Another important element, tackled with these same remote control tools, is the implementation of tracing and certification of the services provided through the use of hardware and software installed on vehicles and the establishment of a Telematic Operational Center.

Table 3.1. Trend of Separate Collection Rate and Waste per Capita and Differences with Provincial and Regional Average.

Year	Population	Separate Collection Rate (%)	Separate Waste Collected per Capita (kg/inh.*year)	Total Waste Pro Capita (kg/inh. *year)
2010	37,571	25	149.26	596.52
2011	36,331	32	182.37	578.84
2012	36,292	35	192.83	558.86
2013	38,121	36	192.06	531.69
2014	38,264	54	260.10	480.42
2015	38,127	578	271.23	469.36
2016	38,145	67	332.51	496.82
2017	38,032	64	298.32	464.12
2018	38,105	67	306.82	461.31
2018	Latina Province	50.67	249.89	493.15
2018	Lazio Region	47.34	243.77	514.92

Source: Our elaborations on ISPRA data.

Table 3.2. Main Economic and Financial Indicators (2015–2018).

	2018	2017	2016	2015
Revenues	7,340,274	6,934,775	6,730,294	4,297,639
EBITDA	521,552	275,319	165,053	116,893
Net Income	55,462	58,721	12,553	7,048
Total Assets	5,229,788	1,887,606	1,872,702	1,851,288
Net Assets	299,884	244,421	185,701	173,149
ROS (%)	2.24	2.21	0.96	1.19
ROA (%)	3.24	8.18	3.52	2.79
ROE (%)	18.49	24.02	6.76	4.07
Debt/Equity ratio	10.52	0.09	0.23	0.03
Debt/EBITDA ratio	6.05	0.08	0.26	0.05
Employees	87	73	54	52

Source: Our elaborations on AIDA data.

During 2017, the Lazio region financed a project involving three main interventions:

(1) The construction of a composting plant serving the green fraction, mowing, and pruning;

(2) The construction of small community composting plants in the three hilly hamlets of Formia, Maranola, Trivio, and Castellonorato;

(3) Interventions aimed at promoting and spreading domestic composting.

Moreover, a project to foster stakeholder engagement and increase user awareness was partly financed by CONAI, a recycling consortium.

Special attention is devoted to tourists. FRZ realized ad hoc information campaigns on how to manage waste and properly separate and collect waste for tourists, living both in hotels and houses, as well as for tourists using beaches and other touristic places on a daily basis.

Owing to a deep drought in summer 2017, it was necessary to refine the system in place by trying to reduce the use of disposable plastic tableware and bottled water. Thus, a large investment was made in 2018 for:

- Fighting against the abandonment of waste: A video surveillance system has been installed, which will be positioned on the municipal territory in different areas from time to time to target and identify any violators;
- User awareness of a better separation of the fractions to obtain minimum quantities of residual dry fraction (undifferentiated);
- Increasing awareness in bathing establishments to better separate waste collection on the beaches managed under concession;
- Awareness of users who use the free beaches of separate waste collection through use of the so-called ecological islands.

Further, control and sanctioning tools were activated in 2018, including a course for agents assessing the sanctions committed regarding waste management. Five company operators held the training course for environmental inspectors and, in collaboration with urban residents, began the operation to repress the most incorrect behavior.

During 2017, along with the strategy of taking on multiple services in the same territory, the strategy of looking for the catchment of synergies and economies of scale and to spread its competencies to other neighboring territories and municipalities started, and in 2017, FRZ was entrusted to carry out the same services for another municipality in the same area, i.e., Ventotene. Then, in 2019, Ventotene became a shareholder along with Formia. Thus, since 2019, FRZ, which changed its name to Futuro Rifiuti Zero ("Zero Waste Future"), has two shareholders: the municipalities of Formia and Ventotene.

Economic and financial results are satisfactory (Table 3.2). After very few years of activity, the publicly owned start-up demonstrated its capability to innovate the waste management service with an efficient model that can realize the needed investment and increase customer satisfaction. Formia residents pay a lower tariff than that of their counterparts in neighboring municipalities, and 92% of Formia residents do not want to come back to the private management model of the past.

Experiences in remunicipalization of urban waste management seem to be positive, both looking at firms that remunicipalized the service several years ago by buying shares from private owners and at start-up firms that demonstrated their ability to realize a sustainable economic and financial path along with very good performance in terms of high separate waste collection rate and low urban waste generation.

The existence of a growing number of start-up cases could lead to a larger number of case studies to be analyzed in future. Although it is embraceable that *remunicipalization could become embroiled in many alternative futures* (Becker et al., 2015, p. 87), the growing number of positive experiences to be shared among policymakers and decision-makers could ease the decision to remunicipalize urban waste management service provision and to share best practices throughout Europe.

This knowledge sharing activity could be fostered by linking positive outcomes from remunicipalization experiences to other urban social movements, such as the ones linked to the ZW or circular economy frameworks, along with the common movements (Becker et al., 2015) that follows the works of Elinor Ostrom (Ostrom, 1990).

4

MEASURING AND COMPARING WASTE MANAGEMENT PERFORMANCE IN AN INTEGRATED VIEW: THE TRIPLE BOTTOM LINE APPROACH TO FOSTER SUSTAINABILITY[1]

ABSTRACT

Chapter 4 focuses on how can we best measure and compare performance of waste management companies, discussing the triple bottom line perspective as a driving approach for public service provision like urban waste management. This approach contributes to extend relevant performance dimensions, broadening its scope to encompass not only cost and efficiency in waste collection and treatment but also environmental and social implications.

Keywords: Waste management utilities; performance; efficiency; triple bottom line; zero waste; sustainability reporting

Measuring and comparing performance of public service provision is of utmost importance to delineate better trends of policy and managerial choices.

In public service provision, the core activity concerns the provision of Services of General Interest (SGIs), granting universality of access and improving quality of life. Indeed, understanding how to measure the performance of public service operators is a relevant topic for municipalities or firms entrusted for public service provision.

1 This chapter was written by Giulia Romano.

The measurement of performance achieved in waste management by municipalities and waste utilities is a thoroughly debated issue among scholars and practitioners worldwide. However, as highlighted by Simões and Marques (2012) after a literature review of studies investigating the economic performance of the waste sector, *despite the importance of the waste sector for local governance, only 107 studies were identified in 45 years of research, which clearly does not reflect the relevance of this matter. Nevertheless, the availability of (reliable) data is fundamental for this kind of research. This might be the most important reason behind the greater number of studies developed about this topic in the last decade. In addition, the increasing awareness of society about environmental issues and the global intention of making the waste service more transparent indicate that the collection of data is the first step* (Simões & Marques, 2012, p. 46).

Data disclosure by waste management operators and local and national government still needs to be improved (Berg & Phillips, 2017), supporting the need of a deeper involvement of the European Union (EU) legislation, e.g., through the forthcoming review of the nonfinancial reporting directive (EU, 2020).

The main issues addressed by literature regarded the waste market structure, ownership, and differences in performance between public and private management models, the impact of incentives in the waste industry, and the use of benchmarking to assess the performance of waste operators and recognize the existing best practices (Simões & Marques, 2012).

In the last few years, a growing number of studies focused on the assessment and analysis of the urban waste management service performance, taking into account some increasingly relevant management aspects of this public service. Along with economic and financial results, variables predicting the environmental impact or service quality also started to be included in the analysis.

Factors affecting the performance of waste operators have been investigated to provide information on how to best define waste policies and waste management sector organization for policymakers and decision-makers.

Population served, population density, and percentage of nonresidential customers are relevant factors affecting efficiency in urban waste management provision (Guerrini, Carvalho, Romano, Cunha Marques, & Leardini, 2017). Further, household features and tourist flows affect efficiency and require adequate consideration when defining urban waste management systems. Finally, tons of waste collected for each load, method adopted (curbside or street bin), and experience reached with a given method, along with political decision (adhesion to zero waste (ZW) strategies and privatization policies), have been investigated to understand their impact on waste management performance (Calabrò & Komilis, 2019; Expósito & Velasco, 2018; Guerrini et al., 2017; Romano, Rapposelli, & Marrucci, 2019; Romano & Molinos-Senante, 2020; Sarra, Mazzocchitti, & Rapposelli, 2017).

Indeed, previous studies highlighted the impact of the context and environment on performance. Therefore, estimating the efficiency of municipalities or waste utilities without taking into account the setting where the service was provided has a limited importance such that policy implications and managerial decisions cannot be taken (Guerrini et al., 2017; Romano, Ferreira, Marques, & Carosi, 2020).

Further, emerging case studies of urban waste management operators demonstrated the relevance of including further data than costs (as inputs) and waste collected and treated (as outputs) in performance assessments. Indeed, empirical studies assessing the efficiency of municipalities in urban waste management (Gastaldi, Lombardi, Rapposelli, & Romano, 2020; Sarra et al., 2017) increasingly use both the amount of waste collected or the infrastructures available, such as collection points or containers, and data regarding recycled waste collected and recyclable rate reached, as output. These data about the waste management service output are used to detail the aim of the service in a circular economy framework and business model, i.e., not only realize a good service in terms of quantity of waste collected and treated but also, and more importantly, to include the real environmental targets to be met (reduction of unsorted waste collected or better a reduction of waste produced tout court and an increase of the rate of separately collected waste to be recycled).

On this matter, Díaz-Villavicencio, Didonet, and Dodd (2017), Guerrini et al. (2017), Sarra et al. (2017), Expósito and Velasco (2018), and Romano and Molinos-Senante (2020) included unsorted waste as an undesirable output to be minimized and a desirable output, i.e., waste from separate collection.

Case studies further highlighted the relevance of considering, along with cost efficiency, further core aspects of urban waste management activities in performance measurement, such as urban waste generation, recycling rate, food waste reduction, landfill rate, ability to obtain revenues from recyclables, tariff applied and its evolution, quality of service provided, energy efficiency, and impact on climate change.

With reference to the quality of service provided, Benito-López, Moreno-Enguix, and Solana-Ibañez (2011) used not only the annual production of residues but also an index built from the survey on the service suitability, called Survey on Local Infrastructures and Equipment, as output in their efficiency analysis of municipalities.

As for another essential public service like drinking water provision (Berg, 2020; D'Inverno, Carosi, & Romano, 2020), composite indicators are needed to evaluate the waste operator performance, encompassing financial and economic results along with environmental sustainability, affordability, and service quality measures (Rigamonti, Sterpi, & Grosso, 2016; D'Inverno et al., 2020). For the waste sector, empirical results could also confirm that benchmarks change if other indicators in addition to economic and financial indicators are considered in the performance analysis. Thus, including other indicators of relevant aspects of the broad mission of waste operators, such as environmental sustainability, affordability, and service quality, changes benchmarking results (D'Inverno et al., 2020).

It appears clear that the performance dimensions to be measured and managed by public service operators, including urban waste management operators, are the ones included in the triple bottom line (TBL) approach, which can reflect economic, social, and environmental performance (Elkington, 1997, 1998). Indeed, according to Elkington, economic prosperity, environmental protection, and social equity should be pursued by firms, and these three aspects should be considered in an integrated way (Elkington, 1997, 1998).

In particular, the provision of public services needs a stronger attention to environmental protection and social equity, owing to the intrinsic nature of the services provided, which are public in nature and relevant for guaranteeing the general interest. Indeed, public services aim at promoting the public good, i.e., prosperity along with social justice and environmental sustainability of communities (Guthrie, Ball, & Farneti, 2010).

This broader TBL approach is in line with the actual and future commitment of the European Commission. With its new Circular Economy Action Plan launched in March 2020, the European Commission supports environmental accounting principles using both financial data and circular economy performance data and foster the inclusion of sustainability criteria into firm policies and strategies (European Commission, 2020a) (Box 4.1 and 4.2).

However, as highlighted by Guthrie et al., *there is a dearth of work that explicitly considers social and environmental management and accounting in*

Box 4.1

Voka Snaga in Ljubljana, Slovenia: Placing Zero Waste (ZW) at the Core of Vision, Mission, and Strategy.

Voka Snaga performs two obligatory public utility services, which clearly set the framework of their mission, with a clear vision: *Being responsible on the way to zero waste society* and becoming *the leading regional company in the field of integrated, sustainable, modern, good-quality and development-oriented management of the most important natural resource – water.* On its website, we can read: *We are a team with a long tradition, which is a good basis for us to become even better by gaining knowledge, experience and wisdom to be able to offer more to the users and make an important contribution to a better tomorrow for us all.*

Regarding waste management, Voka Snaga's mission is: *(1) sustainable waste management in accordance with the ZW strategy and taking care for public (green) areas to ensure a quality living environment; (2) responsible provision of quality customer service for a reasonable price; (3) developing integrated waste management solutions by strengthening long-term partnerships which are in sync with circular economy principles.*

The pay-as-you-throw tariff is calculated only considering unsorted residual waste and organic biological waste, while the other waste fractions are covered through the extended producer responsibility rule. Unsorted and organic waste costs are calculated depending on the bin size and based on the monthly frequency of bin emptying. Tariffs for multiresidential buildings and depend on the bin size, and number of bins, monthly bin collections, household members, and building tenants. In this case (multiresidential buildings), the building manager usually receives the bill and then divides it based on the law or agreements among tenants (Voka Snaga, 2018).

On average, households pay 9.85 €/month, among the lowest in Slovenia (Voka Snaga, 2018). Paper, metal, and batteries are sold by Voka Snaga, and revenues are used to lower tariffs (Voka Snaga, 2018).

public services (Guthrie et al., 2010, p. 451). Further, they pointed out the need for further "theoretical research and in-depth investigations of sustainability practice in public services" (Guthrie et al., 2010, p. 457).

For example, Ball and Grubnic (2007) highlighted the need to extend the research about sustainability in public sector organizations (PSOs) by asking *fundamental questions about the forms of service provision (location, scale, processes of delivery, etc.) that better protect and enhance the life of citizens* (Ball & Grubnic, 2007, p. 257).

Box 4.2

Including Circular Economy in Strategies and Performance Measurement: The LIPOR Experience.

A clear example of including circular economy in its strategies and in performance measurement could be derived from the Greater Porto area in Portugal with LIPOR.

LIPOR, Intermunicipal Waste Management of Greater Porto, is responsible for the management, recovery, and treatment of the municipal waste produced in Porto and other seven associated municipalities: Espinho, Gondomar, Maia, Matosinhos, Póvoa de Varzim, Valongo, and Vila do Conde. LIPOR treats about 520,000 tons of municipal waste per year, produced by about 1,000,000 inhabitants.

LIPOR was founded in 1982 as a Municipalities Association, and it has implemented an integrated waste management, recovered, developed, and built infrastructures since then, as well as organized awareness campaigns for the population.

LIPOR considers waste prevention and the circular business model at the core of its integrated waste management system. The Association of Municipalities supports several initiatives, such as family and community composting, reuse and recycling activities, sustainable public procurement that is incorporated in tender procedures, and environmental training activities to raise awareness of citizens and organizations and to make conscious decisions.

The articulation of policies, strategies, action plans, and respective projects and initiatives, with the Sustainable Development Goals (SDGs), has been one of the LIPOR's drivers. Some examples are highlighted: Education and Environmental Intervention Program, bet on the creation of photovoltaic parks for self-consumption (reducing dependence on nonrenewable sources), Innovation and Research, landscape recovery of environmental liabilities (former dumpsites), strategy to combat climate change, and strategy to promote biodiversity and natural capital.

LIPOR collaborated to the establishment of an Electrical and Electronic Equipment Recovery Centers network (CREW). These centers include educational, training, sustainability, and social areas. Further, CREW spreads knowledge among citizens about available secondhand stores and markets that are all mapped and classified.

LIPOR website also provides a link to the LIPOR Observatory, which is a website with updated statistical information on the management and treatment of municipal waste in the LIPOR area of intervention, providing access to updated and accurate information.

The statistical information available can be segregated by municipality, flow of material, system of collection, type of treatment/final destination, among others. Thus, it allows to create an information management according to user needs. Further, it helps monitoring the goals set for LIPOR and its associated municipalities, additionally providing information on the CO_2 emissions avoided.

Further, for PSOs, *"traditional" bottom line measures of sustainability capture neither the complexity of the challenges that PSOs face nor their role in contributing to higher-level goals of sustainable economies and societies* (Osborne, Radnor, Vidal, & Kinder, 2014, p. 169). Indeed, Eccles, Krzus, Rogers, and Serafeim (2012) highlighted that there are sector-specific sustainability issues that are relevant only, or in a different way, for some sectors and firms operating in them. These differences require specific materiality and reporting standards ad hoc for each industry where similar business models, regulatory standards, and sustainability risks and opportunities are faced.

Applying them at the industry rather than the company level offers a tool for identifying common issues to all firms operating within an industry.

On this matter, it is relevant to highlight the role that sustainability reports could have in reporting, transparency, and stakeholders' engagement of urban waste management operators. Through these reports, firms could explain their scorecards to stakeholders, describing the most relevant indicators used in performance measurement.

The evolution of such indicators could be encouraged by citizens, associations, and regulators. For example, in Portugal, the waste industry regulator, ERSAR, requires a long list of data and indicators from waste operators to be published on its website, realizing a sort of sunshine regulation. As highlighted by Marques, Simões, and Pinto (2018), ERSAR sets, publicly displays, and benchmarks 16 key performance indicators (KPIs), separated into three categories:

(1) Social, considering the protection of users' interests.

(2) Economic, considering the operators' sustainability.

(3) Environment, relating to environmental sustainability.

These KPIs are considered crucial to evaluate all the relevant performance dimensions of waste operators for the regulation perspective, although, as suggested by Marques et al. (2018), room for improvement is always present, for example, by including quality of service among KPIs (Box 4.3).

Box 4.3

Sustainable Reporting: The LIPOR Case.

LIPOR Intermunicipal Waste Management of Greater Porto puts sustainability at the core of its values and strategies and fosters the reduction of waste disposal in landfills, developing an integrated strategy based on four main areas: prevention, multimaterial (such as plastics, paper, and cardboard, glass, metals, waste electrical and electronic equipment (WEEE), others), organic, and energy recovery, which are complemented by a landfill.

LIPOR's strategy is included in an evolution framework for 2021–2030. The evolution is based on four outlines:

(1) Less waste, focusing on efficient resource management, favoring a circular business model.

(2) Less carbon, enhancing the Carbon-Energy Binomial, converging toward decarbonization and the energy transition.

(3) More climate, enhancing our commitment to adapting to climate change.

(4) More biodiversity, increasing the promotion of biodiversity in our context of activity.

These four outlines make up the new strategy for 2021–2030, called the LIPOR 4M strategy – less waste, less carbon, more climate, more biodiversity.
With this strategy, LIPOR aims to achieve a 30% reduction in greenhouse gas emissions in the year 2030.

LIPOR has been publishing its Sustainability Reports since 2004, presenting its economic, environmental, and social performance. The publication of this report for 15 years represents the commitment of LIPOR to the principles of transparency and stakeholder engagement.

LIPOR identifies and prioritizes the most relevant economic, environmental, and social aspects from stakeholders' and firms' perspectives through a Materiality Matrix (Fig. 4.1).

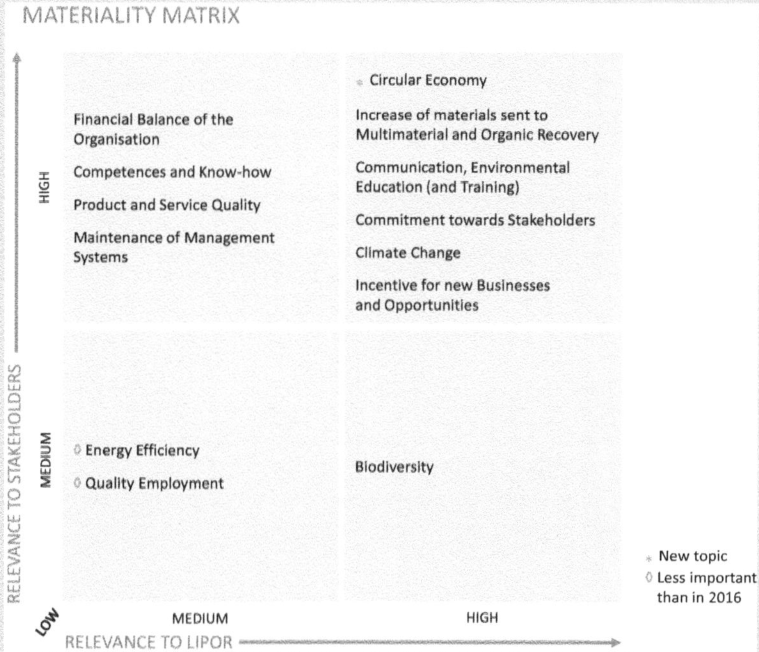

Source: LIPOR's Sustainability Report, 2018.

Fig. 4.1. Materiality Matrix from the Intermunicipal Waste Management of Greater Porto.

LIPOR's targets comprise economic and financial goals, measured through turnover, earnings before interest, taxes, depreciation, and amortization (EBITDA), and net income. However, other relevant targets concern the promotion of biodiversity, fight against greenhouse gas emissions, promotion of knowledge by LIPOR Academy, environmental awareness and education, and strategies for the prevention of waste production.

5

KEY DRIVERS OF SUSTAINABLE URBAN SOLID WASTE MANAGEMENT[1]

ABSTRACT

Chapter 5 deals with key drivers allowing waste management systems to meet circular economy goals, targeting a zero waste approach aimed at eliminating waste and changing the concept of waste into secondary materials. Case studies around Europe highlighted conditions and drivers of sustainable urban solid waste management systems; innovation, responsibility, stakeholder engagement, and knowledge sharing are factors enabling effective and viable urban waste management.

Keywords: Innovation; responsibility; stakeholder engagement; knowledge transfer; sustainability; waste management

Sustainability should be included in the triple bottom line (TBL) approach, i.e., waste management systems should be efficient, effective, and financially autonomous. Further, waste management systems should be able to meet circular economy goals, targeting a zero waste (ZW) approach aimed at eliminating waste and changing the concept of waste into secondary materials. Moreover, urban solid waste management systems should grant adequate service quality and quantity to citizens and for economic activities at affordable prices, while fostering waste generation reduction and increasing recycling activities. Case studies around Europe highlighted the existence of some relevant key drivers that can define sustainable urban solid waste management systems, i.e., innovation, responsibility, stakeholder engagement, and knowledge sharing.

---

1 This chapter was written by Giulia Romano, Claudio Marciano and Maria Silvia Fiorelli.

5.1 INNOVATION[2]

As highlighted by the European Union (EU), *Innovation plays an increasing role in our economy. It provides benefits for citizens as both consumers and workers. It is essential for creating better jobs, building a greener society, and improving our quality of life but also for maintaining EU competitiveness in the global market* (European Parliament, 2020).

An operational definition of innovation has been coined within innovation studies, a transdisciplinary research field born in the 80s, when the impact of globalization and increasing demand personalization contributed to strengthen the strategic perception of innovative skills (Van de Ven, 1999). Innovation is defined as an intentional application of ideas, processes, products, and procedures, novel in relation to the unit of adoption, and oriented toward the production of a benefit (Rogers, 2003; West & Farr, 1990). Several authors (Colaianni, 2008) have highlighted how this definition separates the concept of innovation from that of creativity, indicating how innovation is a distinct phenomenon, as it always implies a practical development aimed at achieving a tangible benefit through appropriate as well as original actions. Therefore, innovation is a widespread phenomenon in organizational contexts of different scale and complexity and is incorporated in a variety of devices, i.e., products and services, but also processes and cultural orientations.

Innovation is a process, rather than a single output or an isolated cognitive competence (Rogers, 2003). Most models described in literature propose a linear vision, consisting of an ordered series of phases, within which rational schemes of action prevail (Dyer, Gregersen, & Christensen, 2011). Therefore, innovative behavior would take place in three sequential phases: (1) generation of the idea, i.e., the associative process leading to the elaboration of a solution; (2) search for consensus, i.e., discussion of the idea with the organizational group of references and financiers, considering the risks and opportunities of its implementation; and (3) implementation, i.e., where the idea gives rise to a prototype followed by experimentation and, if successful, practical application.

This approach has received some criticism (De Jong & Den Hartog, 2008; Del Torre, 2008), indicating the presence of other phases in addition to those described and questioning the linearity of the process, which is incapable of rendering the dynamics of conflict and tension that emerge from research carried out in the field. Van de Ven (1999) discussed how the innovation

2 The section was written by Giulia Romano and Claudio Marciano. The authors contributed equally.

process would be animated by two antithetical tensions: the divergent one, in which skills and behaviors are exploratory and experimentation is free, and the convergent one, in which synthetic and rationalizing attitudes and actions prevail. Therefore, the innovative process would be cyclical and autopoietic, without a necessary temporal sequentiality between the individual phases and without variables intervening in isolation in each of phases.

This theoretical pattern is relevant in describing the key drivers of excellent urban solid waste management, i.e., the required innovation involves product, process, marketing, and organizational aspects, and should put waste operators at the frontiers of international managerial and technical best practices, expanding beyond habits and most widespread routines.

Innovation in waste management first requires committed policymaking in waste reduction and recycling, along with activism at local and national levels. As illuminated by the Capannori experience (Connett, 2013), highly motivated and committed activists fighting against incineration could attract the attention of a growing number of citizens and then, of local policymakers. The latter are the driving forces for introduction of innovative ideas at the local level to overcome existing waste management problems, introducing different approaches and fostering the realization of needed plants for recycling and composting.

Indeed, the political commitment exploited through the adoption of the ZW strategy at the municipality level can foster an increase in the collection rate of separated waste, highlighting how this political decision is not mere political posturing. Instead, as highlighted by Romano, Rapposelli, and Marrucci (2019), Romano, Ferreira, Marques, and Carosi (2020), it can be a key driver for significantly improving economic and environmental results.

From this perspective, innovation consists of both the ability to delegitimize existing solutions, exploring their contradictions and shortcomings, and propose an alternative management system, with consistent objectives and concrete feasible practices. In our case, innovation is achieved by applying door-to-door collection or domestic composting, not because of the originality of these practices, rather because they are "new" for the territories experiencing these practices.

Innovation always has to face several barriers. Case studies demonstrated that innovation in waste management was frequently blocked by several factors, from illegal activities and conflict of interests to legal practices that prefer to manage public services "as usual," avoiding the introduction of novel approaches based more on mere political posturing than on good practice examples or scientific results. Innovation can reduce costs owing to inefficiencies or avoidable risks. Regarding the importance of logistics in defining waste trucks routes, investments in technologies and mapping activities can reduce medium- to long-term costs, and developing the most efficient routes can significantly reduce costs in terms of labor, fuel, and vehicles. Further, innovation in creating risk management systems will reduce risks of accidents at work of the waste collection workers by introducing newly framed trucks, with doors opening on the sidewalk instead of the traditional ones opening on the streets (Minoja & Romano, 2021) (Box 5.1).

Box 5.1

Innovation in Service Organization and Tariff Setting: The Case of ASCIT and Capannori

ASCIT SpA in Capannori is well known for the pioneering adoption of the curbside "door-to-door" collection method in all municipalities served and for the application of pay-as-you-throw. In 2017, according to data from the regional resource recovery company (ARRR), the percentage of separate waste collection achieved in the six municipalities served was 82.4% on average, against a regional average of 53.89%.

The categories of waste collected at home are:

(1) Paper and cardboard
(2) Organic
(3) Glass
(4) Lightweight multimaterial
(5) Nonrecyclable waste
(6) Diapers
(7) Oil and vegetable fats
(8) Mowing and pruning

In particular, for those who perform domestic composting, thus not contributing to door-to-door collection, a 20% reduction is recognized on the variable part of the tariff. All the door-to-door containers, the composter, and bags are supplied free of charge by ASCIT at the authorized counters and prepared in such a manner that the harvest operator can easily distinguish any errors at the time of collection. In the municipalities where punctual tariffs are active, the gray bags for the undifferentiated waste are equipped with microchips and can only be delivered to the citizens by the Ecosportello. On the days indicated in the calendar, citizens are required to expose the waste outside the home by 7 a.m. or after 10 p.m. of the previous day. If the operator identifies waste that is not suitable or not properly supplied, he will put a red stamp on the bag to inform the user of the error and the failure to take the material. In fact, the ASCIT operator can only collect waste correctly delivered. By regulation and for safety reasons, users must only use the bags and bins supplied by ASCIT, and the material must be delivered inside the bins or bags and must not be left loose or on the ground. Otherwise, the operator is mandated to not collect the waste.

ASCIT performs free home collection up to 2 m^3 or three pieces for bulky and waste of electrical and electronic equipment (WEEE; by appointment). However, citizens can directly provide bulky and WEEE to collection centers available in the area based on the municipality of residence. The collection centers can receive the following materials:

(1) Timber (furniture and more)

(2) Metal (bed nets, railings, and more)

(3) Mowing and pruning (gardening)

(4) Appliances (from the light bulb to the refrigerator at home)

(5) Batteries, paints, dirty containers

(6) Building material (bricks, tiles, and ceramics)

(7) Bulky waste

(8) Oil and edible fats

The conferment to collection centers is encouraged through a scoring system applied on the basis of the quantity assigned and the type of material. On reaching 500 points, € 20 are deducted from the invoice.

The collection of mowing and pruning takes place on set days, but it can be collected at home for larger quantities by appointment and on payment.

ASCIT has obtained the certifications UNI EN ISO 37001 "Anti-Corruption Management System," UNI EN ISO 9001 regarding quality, BS OHSAS 18001 concerning health and safety, and UNI EN ISO 14001 on environmental matters.

The tariff foreseen in four of the six municipalities managed by ASCIT is calculated based on the square meters of the house and the number of components (domestic users) or the product category to which they belong (nondomestic users). Contrastingly, the pay-as-you-throw tariff was introduced some time ago in two of the six municipalities managed and is based on the "more separation less pay" principle and, therefore, calculated based on the quantity of unsorted waste produced in the variable part.

The punctual rate consists of a fixed part and a variable part, i.e., for each sack of undifferentiated waste withdrawn, the user is billed the amount of approximately € 10. The user pays depending on the number of bags delivered and not on their weight. To cover the cost of the service, each user is in any case required to pay the variable fee based on at least the minimum number of undifferentiated waste bags conferred to avoid encouraging the abandonment of waste and/or the incorrect conferment of nondifferentiable waste. Currently, the quality of transfer in the municipalities managed by ASCIT of the light multimaterial is high, with only approximately 15% of average impurities.

Data show that the citizens served by the punctual tariff are particularly virtuous, requiring a lower than minimum emptying frequency.

The punctual tariff pursues the following objectives:

(1) To incentivize lower production of undifferentiated waste due to shrewd purchases from the environmental point of view (the less waste produced, the lesser you pay);

(2) To incentivize better separate collection (better the separation, the lesser you pay);

(3) Greater tariff equality for users (tariff customization based on the polluter pays principle);

(4) Greater business efficiency in the collection (optimization of collection rounds).

Comparing the tariffs applied in 2012 with the specific tariffs applied in 2018, a reduction emerges for all user types (size of buildings and number of family members), ranging from 5% to 14% (Table 5.1).

Table 5.1. Rates Applied in 2012 and 2018 by ASCIT by User Type.

Square Meters	Household Members	Rates 2012	Rates 2018 with Minimum Number of Collections	Diff. 2018–2012 (in Euro)	Diff. 2018–2012 (in %)
50	1	73	70	−3	−5%
70	2	144	123	−21	−14%
100	3	213	188	−25	−12%
140	4	287	248	−39	−14%

Source: ASCIT.

Moreover, the empirical evidence shows that the tariffs applied by ASCIT are extremely competitive if compared with those applied in other municipalities and other provinces of Tuscany. The province of Lucca appears to be, on average, the one with the highest separate waste collection percentage in Tuscany and the third for average rate, after Florence and Siena.

To adopt the pay-as-you-throw tariff, ASCIT has identified the necessary technology, and in particular:

(1) A management software;

(2) A method of conferment by users;

(3) A hardware and software technology for the punctual detection of contributions.

In particular, the bags for the undifferentiated waste have been equipped with a preapplied radio-frequency identification (RFID) tag. Therefore, garbage collection vehicles must be equipped with an RFID microprocessor control system. Data collection is done by automatically sending information from the collection vehicles to a central server that feeds a database, on the basis of which tariff is applied.

Starting from January 2019, through the citizen-user portal available on the ASCIT website (www.ascit.it), it is possible to check the number of nonrecyclable nonseparated waste withdrawals and the dates of conferment, from the comfort of the customers' home.

Innovation could be fostered by law and regulation, which could raise the need to change existing processes, generate new technical solutions, and modify habits at both waste operator and stakeholder levels. As highlighted by Cecere and Corrocher (2016), regulation can positively affect innovation, even if there is an optimal level of regulation after which there is no improvement in fostering innovation.

The tariff system could be an effective driver of innovation for both waste utilities and citizen behavior, e.g., the role of the PAYT tariff mechanism in fostering virtuous conducts.

Innovation in waste management also means to improve waste treatment plants availability and their compliance with existing best practice, using cutting-edge technologies.

The example of Milan in the north of Italy in the 90s is significant. The waste crisis was solved by realizing cutting-edge waste treatment plants and avoiding the use of a privately owned and managed landfill, which had been used intensively until then. The waste management system, implemented through participative processes, involving several civic associations and all the relevant stakeholders allowed the realization of cutting-edge plants in a short period of time, ensuring self-sufficiency in waste treatment for Milan, the second largest Italian city, creating the opportunity to exploit the benefits of door-to-door collection and the great involvement and engagement of citizens and firms.

In Italy, the waste management company of the Treviso area in Veneto called Contarina SpA realized a collaboration with Fater SpA, an Italian company (joint venture between Procter & Gamble and Angelini Group) that built the first industrial plant worldwide that recycles used baby diapers and other personal absorbent products to obtain plastics, cellulose, and super absorbent polymer – all secondary raw materials that can be employed for several applications and industries. In this context, the urban waste utility is involved in the separate collection of personal absorbent products from the users to avoid the creation of waste from baby diapers, feminine pads, and products for incontinence. This will fulfill several goals, i.e., a reduction of waste to be treated and consequently, a reduction in treatment costs and thus, tariffs for citizens as well as a reduction in waste production, reducing the environmental impact. The innovation was substantial, as personal absorbent products represent between 2% and 7% of municipal solid waste in Europe (Arena, Ardolino, & Di Gregorio, 2016), and in recent years, they were considered as nonrecyclable waste (Box 5.2).

Another example is the renounce to build an incineration plant of a European capital, Ljubljana, in Slovenia. To foster waste reduction and

Box 5.2

Innovation in Waste Management through Collaboration and Knowledge Sharing: The Circular Economy Example of Contarina SpA

Contarina SpA is a cutting-edge waste management utility of the Province of Treviso in the Veneto Region, northeast part of Italy. Contarina has a strong commitment to reduce waste production and increase recycling rate. It is considered one of the top waste utilities in Italy and Europe, and it received several prices and recognitions for its efforts in realizing outstanding results in sustainable waste management.

In 2018, Contarina performed 88.8% of separate collection rate compared with 74% and 56% in Veneto Region and Italy, respectively, and only 57 kg of unsorted waste per capita compared with 125 and 225 kg in Veneto and Italy, respectively (Contarina Spa, 2019).

Contarina has a recognized experience in innovation and knowledge creation and sharing. It realized several knowledge management activities in collaboration with partners to develop innovative waste management systems that can foster efficiency and effectiveness, e.g., ad hoc trucks to reduce drivers' risks, devices to increase truck route efficiency, or systems for applying pay-as-you-throw tariffs with devices to track waste bags. Further, Contarina collaborated with Fater SpA, an Italian company, born as a joint venture between Procter & Gamble and Angelini Group. Fater manufactures and distributes personal hygiene with brand products such as Pampers, LINES, and Tampax. The collaboration regarded the construction of an innovative recycling plant to treat and recycle absorbent personal products, from baby diapers to feminine pads and incontinence products.

The plant, located close to Contarina, transforms used absorbent products, separately collected by Contarina staff, into precious secondary raw materials, i.e., plastics, cellulose, and super absorbent polymer.

This innovative plant can reduce waste production and increase recycling rate, by avoiding to incinerate or landfill products that were considered as unrecyclable before.

The plant made the treatment possible at industrial scale (up to 10,000 t of used absorbent products per year), serving a population of about 1,000,000 people. Based on Contarina's data, absorbent products were 29% of mixed waste in 2015 and 27% in 2016. Thus, recycling absorbent products will significantly reduce mixed waste treated by Contarina and increase recycling rates in the municipalities served. Further, it highlighted the relevance of a deep analysis of mixed waste to exploit innovation efforts mostly on projects that can significantly reduce waste and increase recycling rates.

recycling, Ljubljana realized an innovative recycling plant. Further, it realized strong and effective communication activities, fostering reuse centers and creating and managing an innovative recycling plant.

Voka Snaga, the Slovenian waste utility, could reach outstanding waste reduction and recycling rates in a very short period of time, demonstrating that with a strong commitment, it is possible to change citizens habits through innovations in marketing and communication, tariff setting methods that foster and value virtuous behaviors, and supporting technological innovation in waste management. The results also included a drastic reduction in landfill use (Box 5.3).

The availability of treatment plants is increasingly relevant, as waste treatment costs are raising, and municipalities and firms need to have proper instruments to close the cycle in a circular economy approach.

Mixed waste could be separated in ad hoc treatment plants to obtain as many recyclable materials as possible. In contrast, organic waste treatment plants could generate compost to be used in agriculture and urban green.

Box 5.3

RCERO Ljubljana – Innovate Plants to Recover Materials from Biological and Unsorted Waste

RCERO Ljubljana is an innovative and self-sufficient recycling plant that, in very few years, helped Slovenia to reach high targets of recycling, reducing landfill to a relatively small role. It generates its own energy and processes seemingly useless mix waste in recyclable materials or fuel, so that less than 5% of residual waste produced by 59 Slovenian municipalities (around one-third of Slovenian waste) ends up in a landfill. It is effectively organized, i.e., when waste arrives at the plant in trucks, it is unloaded into one of two buildings each of a different color: the orange facilities process organic waste, while the green facilities process mixed waste. Mixed waste first proceeds to a shredder, from where it goes to a sieve that separates it according to size. From the sieve, it travels on conveyor belts separators above them, separating waste based on its characteristics. All separated materials proceed to the recycling facilities. Unrecyclable materials are converted into a fuel that has a similar calorific value to brown coal. All processes are coordinated from the control room, where supervisors monitor the entire plant using cameras.

First, biological waste is sieved. Small particles are prepared for the bioreactor, while larger organic waste first proceeds to shredding and then to further sieving. In the bioreactor, the waste undergoes anaerobic fermentation similar to that in the stomach of ruminants. This generates biogas, which is in turn used to generate electricity and heat. The biomass that leaves the bioreactor is pressed, dry aerated, and left to mature to prepare compost of the highest quality.

RCERO Ljubljana is a global example of regional integration and cooperation. It renews natural resources, completes the consumer cycle, and integrates repurposing and craft workshops.

Innovative approaches are still needed to force citizens to provide only accurately separated organic waste, allowing the preparation of high-quality compost, certified to be used safely in agriculture. Further, organic waste treatment plants generate biogas to be used for the self-sufficiency of the plant itself and further (Box 5.4).

Box 5.4

The Relevance of Waste Treatment Plants Today: Italian Examples of Costs Impact

A good management model of separate waste collection and treatment is essential. This is also because the rates of treatment/disposal of the different fractions of separate collection have increased in the last years, especially those of unsorted waste. For example, for Formia Rifiuti Zero (FRZ), located in Lazio, beginning from the assignment date of the waste collection and disposal service in 2015, unpredictable increases have been detected. The disposal rate of residual dry waste, which was 89.51 €/t in 2015, progressively increased to 100.07, 124.74, 126.11, up to 138.14 €/t in 2016, 2017, 2018, and 2019, respectively (net of ecotax and environmental benefits when due, in addition to the annual monetary revaluation according to the ISTAT index). This increase significantly impacted the performance of waste utilities and, thus, affected the tariff paid by citizens.

The costs of treating organic waste also increased, from 105.00 to 160.00 €/t in in 2015 and 2018, respectively. These data highlighted the importance of owning the organic waste treatment plants to avoid the yearly fluctuation of costs.

As stated in the 2018 ASCIT annual report, *since January 2018, China has closed its borders to various types of waste to be recycled, from plastic to paper to the slag of steel processing and industry waste textile; the immediate consequences were the multiplication of the waste storage warehouses, often subject to fires, and the increase over 70% of the prices to use the waste-to-energy plants, in addition to the drastic reduction in the demand and the price of some recyclable waste (in particular paper and light multi-material) and the contraction of revenues deriving from their sale*. ASCIT has signed agreements with some important companies to efficiently and conveniently dispose of separately collected waste. In particular, an agreement was signed with the company SMURFIT KAPPA for the disposal of the joint and mixed paper. ASCIT has signed an agreement with the company Fertitalia Srl for the organic fraction of collected waste. Moreover, the light multimaterial is sold to Revet SpA. Finally, for the disposal of bulky waste and mixed packaging from nondomestic users and from 2019, for the disposal of light multimaterial, ASCIT has signed an agreement with Valfreddana Recuperi Srl.

In contrast, regarding undifferentiated waste, ASCIT disposes of the waste collected in the plant managed by AAMPS SpA (Livorno) and partly in the selection and composting plant (TMB) of Pioppogatto in the municipality of Massarosa managed by the company ERSU SpA.

In the Porto area, in 2019, LIPOR was considered a "Nonbusiness Entity of the Research and Innovation System (ENESII) by the ANI (National Innovation Agency) in Portugal." LIPOR and the eight associated municipalities reached the highest ever value in recycling owing to the strong investment developed to maximize and increase the amount of materials sent for recycling. In that area, citizens have a system of infrastructure at their disposal, equipment, and services for waste selective delivery (civic amenity sites, bring bank system, and selective door-to-door collection areas), a set of special collection services, and the Sorting Plant and Support Platforms, where waste sorted by citizens undergoes a further detailed sorting activity to be subsequently sent to the recycling industries (Box 5.5).

Similarly, innovation in plant availability allowed the Helsinki area in Finland and Ljubljana area in Slovenia to achieve near zero landfilled waste.

Box 5.5

Innovation at LIPOR

Innovation is a strategic theme for LIPOR, and its implementation is based on three different areas: managing innovation, researching and developing new products, and innovation. Indeed, LIPOR's long-term perspective for innovation is to consolidate relationships with stakeholders. Innovation is defined as *Thinking creatively, facing situations from different perspectives, finding new and effective solutions for different kinds of issues, redesigning processes, tackling new challenges creatively, and shifting paradigms are the drive and motivation for Innovation at LIPOR.*

LIPOR was the first certified entity in the Portuguese waste sector for Research, Development, and Innovation (NP 4457 standard), and has a "Research, Development, and Innovation Unit (UIDI)"; according to its sustainability report, UIDI *primarily aims to promote value creation within the Organisation. This goal is to be achieved through two components: the promotion of an Innovation Culture across the entire Organisation (Innovation Management) and the implementation of Projects that generate added value (Innovation).*

The main ongoing projects, focused on a circular economy approach, include the digitization of operational processes, the recovery of slag from the waste-to-energy plant, the development of new products for agriculture, and the development of a recovery line for rigid plastics (nonpackaging).

LIPOR uses COTEC's Innovation Scoring to measure innovation, using the management system as a tool that enhances innovation and adds value to the organization.

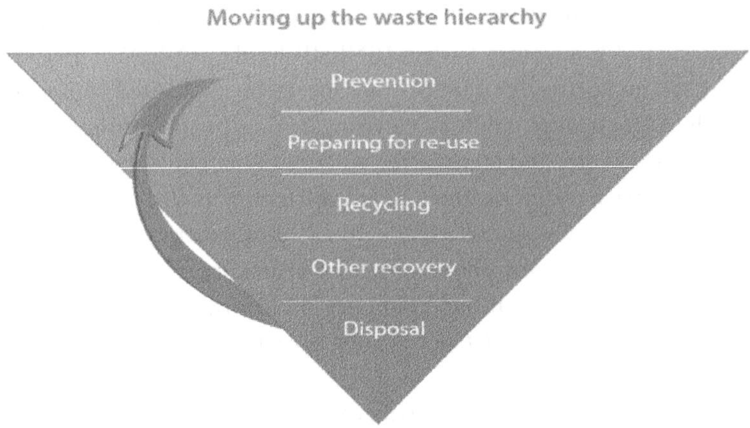

Source: EU (2010), Being wise with waste: the EU's approach to waste management.

Fig. 5.1. European Union's Waste Hierarchy.

However, in policymaking and innovation activity, it is essential to consider the waste hierarchy defined by the EU. Although disposal into landfill is considered the worst solution, we should point out that recycling must precede other recovery choices. Thus, strategies and investments should prioritize prevention, preparation for reuse, and recycling. Recycling plants are essential to reduce the need to find other recovery solutions, including energy recovery and landfill (Fig. 5.1).

5.2 RESPONSIBILITY[3]

Responsibility is one of the keys for successful urban waste management. It needs to be shared and extended from the policy and managerial level to household and nonhousehold customers. Indeed, at source (by households or in organizations), waste should be managed, separated, and properly prepared for collection. Through proper information and explanation, but also with the help of laws, rules, sanctions, and extended and accurate controls, citizens and organization should take part in the responsibility of correctly managing waste to reduce, compost, and recycle them.

Responsibility becomes a driver of creation of best practices, when it is shared among policymakers, waste operators, and citizens in a virtuous circle of relationships. In this context, citizens have a crucial role regarding their behavior, such that policymakers and waste operators could provide

3 The section was written by Giulia Romano.

appropriate and effective support in order to create different habits, resulting in a deeper acceptance of responsibility.

Managing urban waste is a matter of all stakeholders in a modern community, and responsibility should be the basic common value supporting the community itself.

The cases of Capannori in Tuscany and of Milan in the mid-90s are exemplary. Capannori, a virtuous small Italian municipality for waste management activities, led the ZW revolution in Italy and then in Europe, owing to the concurrent presence of a visionary environmental activist, a young environment alderman, and a public waste management utility that could put policy ideas into practice, in a virtuous interchange among policymakers and public managers.

In Milan, the separate waste collection rate grew from 5% to 35% in a few weeks (Ganapini, 2004) by concurrently projecting an integrated system of urban waste management that included a well-projected door-to-door separate collection system, self-sufficient waste management plants to treat and recycle unsorted and organic waste, and an active involvement of all relevant civic, industrial, and environmental local associations.

The Milan case in the 90s (see paragraph 2.3.1), concerning a big, innovative, touristic, and service and industrial leading city in Europe, highlighted the possibility of implementing good waste management practices also in complex contexts and in relatively short time. It also underlined the relevance of committed policymakers for enforcing big changes in urban waste management; their presence and activity can attract and retain the most suited managers and project leaders in publicly owned utilities, i.e., committed, independent, professional, and influential people, who can realize and implement innovative projects to be then spread around Italy and Europe.

Further, the case of Milan stressed the role played by citizens, firms, and civil society in realizing big changes in habits to meet sustainable targets that can reduce environmental impact and increase well-being.

The Contarina model is based on the concept of responsibility that is needed both at individual and collective levels (see paragraph 5.3.2). Citizens have an "individual responsibility" in sorting waste correctly at source and then respecting the fixed calendar for door-to-door collection, while Contarina has the "collective responsibility" in the waste collection, transport, treatment, and recovery for recycling, as promised to the municipalities served and to citizens through direct communication and formal and informal interaction.

According to the Contarina's framework, this responsibility, individual and collective, should be translated into actions that then imply outcomes, such as lower tariffs, higher quantity of recyclables, and lower quantity of mixed waste requiring treatment.

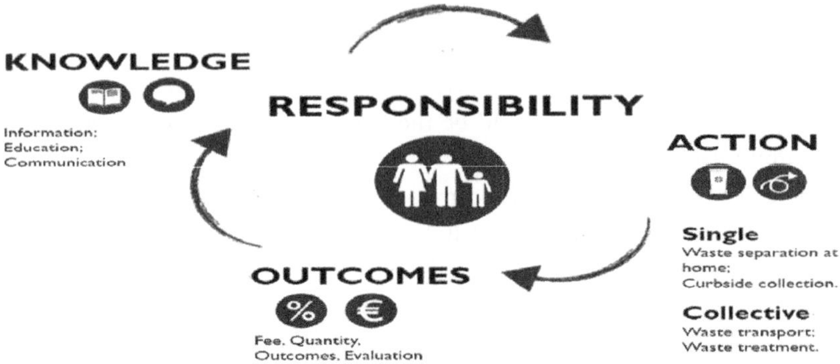

Source: Contarina SpA (2019).

Fig. 5.2. The Responsibility Framework of Contarina.

Information, education, and communication activities are relevant in fostering individual responsibility, as well as in creating among employees, managers, and shareholders the due commitment in strategies and targets defined (Fig. 5.2).

From the waste operator side, responsibility means facilitating:

- Separation at source, through clear information with easily available dedicated brochure, website, etc;
- Collection of separated waste;
- Recovering waste collected properly, fostering reuse, recycling, and composting (Box 5.6).

This includes the need to involve all employees in the firm vision and strategic plan realization, from managers and truck drivers to waste collection operators and communication managers and staff.

ASCIT involved all employees in its organizational change, e.g., it trusted its mechanical workers and provided them new responsibilities; instead of externalizing the maintenance services through long-term rentals that included maintenance in the rent, the service was entrusted to the ASCIT workshop employees. Internalization significantly saved costs (fewer spare parts for trucks and machines and less extraordinary maintenance) and increased job creation (from three to six mechanicals in the following years).

Further, with reference to EU, it has been affirmed that *in the Member States where organised crime poses considerable problems, corruption is often used as a facilitator* (European Commission, 2014a, p. 19) and that *construction linked to urban development, as well as waste management are among the sectors most prone to corruption at local level* (European Commission, 2014a, p. 19). A case study about Naples highlighted the relevance of policy implementation considering social, economic, and financial impacts of good urban waste management. Critical issues in governance and managerial practices, infrastructures, as well as corruption and organized crime were highlighted as relevant barriers to correct policy implementation (BIO Intelligence Service, 2011b).

Organized crime is increasingly interested in managing waste without respecting law and regulation, also owing to the increasing treatment cost. Improper collection, transport, recovery, or disposal of waste are considered environmental crimes as they can cause significant harm or risk to the environment and human health (Europol, 2020). As observed by the Italian National Anti-Corruption Authority (ANAC), the procedures for entrusting services relating to the waste cycle are characterized by a high economic impact. Thus, they are highly susceptible to negative repercussions for the community and to attract, as confirmed by numerous events, the interests of criminal organizations, often of mafia type (ANAC, 2019). Both in-house providers and public tenders have been under scrutiny by ANAC, finding that there could be opportunities for maladministration and fraud in both cases (ANAC, 2019). Indeed, as highlighted by Schleifer and Vishny, *with full corruption, neither commercialization nor privatization matters*; thus *in principle, there is no magic line that separates firms from politicians once they are privatized* (Schleifer & Vishny, 1994).

To foster responsibility, information availability is needed for decision-makers, both households and companies or other organizations. Data availability, such as through benchmarking tools, is useful as it allows proper decision-making, based on accurate information (Box 5.7).

5.3 STAKEHOLDER ENGAGEMENT[4]

Stakeholder engagement is a continuous process through which people, who may be affected by the decisions of an organization or can influence the implementation of its decisions, are involved in the decision-making process itself. Indeed, stakeholders may support or oppose the decisions, thus concurring to the success or failure of a strategy, a project, or the

4 The section was written by Giulia Romano and Maria Silvia Fiorelli. The authors contributed equally.

Box 5.6

Residents' Waste Management in the Helsinki Metropolitan Area

Helsinki Region Environmental Services Authority (HSY) made delivering daily waste to the correct places as easy as possible. Indeed, in the Helsinki area, recoverable waste (packages such as metals, plastics, and carton) and mixed waste generated by households can be taken to the waste containers in the properties' waste facilities or to a Rinki eco take-back point located in the respective area.

- Clothes and other items still fit for use can be taken, e.g., to the Helsinki Metropolitan Area Reuse Centre.
- Electric devices are received for free at Sortti Stations and by collection vehicles touring every year. Shops selling electric equipment also receive small-size electric devices.
- Hazardous waste is received free of charge by collection vehicles, which tour every year, and at the Sortti Station, or they can be disposed of in collection containers for hazardous waste, dozens of which are located throughout the Helsinki Metropolitan Area and in Kirkkonummi.
- Households' medicinal waste is collected from pharmacies where customers return their old medicines.
- Renovation waste, brushwood, garden waste, and small loads of other waste types (e.g. textile waste since 2020) are received at Sortti Stations. Certain waste types are free of charge, some subject to charge. They must be sorted according to the waste type.

The Sortti pick-up service is an order service delivering large and broken items to a Sortti Station. It is subject to a charge of € 60–120, and the order can be electronically placed. The pick-up service can be ordered for items still in good condition, which will then be delivered to the Helsinki Metropolitan Reuse Centre.

Everyone can also deliver these items by themselves to a Sortti Station after payment.

Box 5.7

Petra Waste Benchmarking in Helsinki

Petra Waste Benchmarking was a freely available tool created by the Helsinki Region Environmental Services Authority (HSY) for companies and organizations to report their waste data since 2003. It was recently replaced with other cooperation systems for gathering statistics, which completed the Petra data.

The tool provided companies an approximation of how their waste amounts compare to others from the same sector and calculated the approximate CO_2 emissions caused by the company's waste management. The data of an individual workplace were confidential but were used by HSY for statistics. Indeed, Petra Waste Benchmarking was used by HSY to collect data of the municipal solid waste not collected by HSY, i.e., waste similar to household waste collected by private companies from businesses and organizations. The data were used by HSY to calculate the total municipal solid waste amount and recycling rate in the Helsinki Region.

At best, some 600 businesses and organizations reported their waste amount to the Petra Waste Benchmarking system.

The waste report included reporting of the waste amount produced per employee, and the results were used to calculate a waste coefficient: kilogram produced per person-year for each sector. Using regional personnel statistics combined with this coefficient, HSY got an approximate amount of waste produced by each sector.

Every two years, HSY awarded one company or public entity that succeeded in significantly reducing its waste amounts. With this award, HSY wanted to encourage companies to monitor the waste amount they generate and to take actions to reduce waste generation.

implementation of a relevant innovation. They can influence the organization of the waste operator and the community served, by supporting or opposing the decisions about the waste reduction projects, collection methods such as the door-to-door suggested by the ZW framework, separation at source, implementation of tariff setting methods, and so on.

In public service provision, stakeholders need to be involved and listened to, as they are affected in the long term by relevant waste management decisions, such as the creation of treatment plants in the territory where they live and operate, or by the collection method chosen (i.e., door-to-door or street bins).

The relevance of community's unwillingness to accept waste treatment plants, such as the "Not In My Backyard" (NIMBY) syndrome, is demonstrated by successful activist campaigns, both currently and in past years

(Srivastava, Kulshreshtha, Mohanty, Pushpangadan, & Singh, 2005; Sun, Yung, Chan, & Zhu, 2016). Further, inefficiencies or mistakes in programming and managing the urban waste service will affect stakeholders through tariffs that reflect those inefficiencies and mistakes, along with eventual sanctions applied by the law.

Formal stakeholder consultations complement a broader interaction with stakeholders through a multitude of opportunities to meet, exchange ideas, and dialog.

As highlighted by the Contarina and Capannori case studies, public managers and politicians such as mayors or aldermen are directly involved in meetings with citizens and associations to explain the innovations planned, clarify the targets to be met, and describe opportunities for increasing quality of services, reducing environmental impacts, creating new jobs, and social opportunities, such as the ones through reuse centers managed by municipalities or waste operators.

Municipalities and waste firms wishing to increase recycling and reducing waste production put lots of efforts in stakeholder engagement, through communication and training activities.

Communication is essential to: (1) inform citizens on the goals pursued by municipalities and waste utilities mission and strategic plans, (2) motivate people to reduce waste production and increase recycling activities, (3) advise individuals and firms on how to best separate waste at source and prepare them for door-to-door collection, and (4) foster citizens' attention on the waste issue.

Waste operators should communicate using different media, including increasingly relevant social media. Cutting-edge waste firms use specialized staff for their communication activities. Communication staff members are experts in communication and training; however, communication staff also includes environmental specialists, and both competences are needed to reach expected goals.

Relevant experiences show that innovation in communication is essential to overcome usual communication limits and reach all expected targets using traditional but also innovative approaches and instruments. For example, HSY in Helsinki area offers classes for schools and day-care centers on waste reduction, waste sorting, and circular economy, along with other innovative ways to create opportunities of dialog, with specific targets needing special attention (Box 5.8).

Similarly, in Ljubljana, the communication staff of Voka Snaga realized several innovative communication initiatives to engage stakeholders in the corporate vision and mission, e.g., to reduce waste generation, they avoided

Box 5.8

Communication and Training in Helsinki Area

Each year, Helsinki Region Environmental Services Authority (HSY) realizes advisory classes for adults and immigrants and workshops and education sessions for children in the Helsinki area in Finland, including classes on reduction of waste for 5–6-year-olds.

In 2019, the Ämmässuo Eco-Industrial Centre and Sortti Stations had 1,759 visitors. Further, HSY provides illustrated sorting guides and instructions in several languages, working in cooperation with institutions and associations such as the Finnish Refugee Council. Additionally, all sorting guides for all waste types in all languages are available online to help citizens understand how to best separate waste.

HSY is promoting waste sorting campaigns under the umbrella project "Thank you for Sorting your Waste." The campaign targets especially young adults, as HSY research has shown that they are surprisingly passive in sorting their waste. Thus, HSY cooperated with a celebrity to spread the message in video advertisements and social media.

Recently, HSY used a Waste Escape Room to attract visitors using innovative ways to provide sorting advice, e.g., an escape room game that requires players to solve recycling and waste sorting related problems, which was built in a container and is played by about four people for a maximum of 15 minutes. Additionally, an information point was set up alongside the Waste Escape Room, also especially directed to young adults, to provide residents with waste sorting tips, biowaste bags, and "Thank you for sorting your waste" campaign bags.

Eight popular events hosted the HSY escape room throughout the summer and reached about 10,000 people, directing attention to the novel approach to advice through promotion in social media and through influencers as well as traditional media.

the use of traditional communication by firm staff, but realized a communication campaign via the rubbish bins located throughout the city center. The bins spoke through comics highlighting the importance of creating as little new waste as possible.

This innovative communication reduces the distrust of stopping at traditional information desks. In fact, Voka Snaga noted a higher curiosity and interest in reading the comics on the rubbish bins compared to that in traditional communication activities.

Training activities allowed to share acquired knowledge with interested people wishing to take part in classes, workshops, seminars, conferences, or other events about acquiring information, replicating managerial models, introducing innovation, and improving results. In training activities, codified knowledge is shared with different targets, from children in schools to managers and activists.

For waste operators, it is increasingly relevant to open their plants, allow to visit them, look directly at operations, and make people aware of the results of their sorting activities. Direct visits also allow to increase awareness of technology innovation results regarding automation of most activities in waste treatment, high security in waste management, odor reduction, and real circular economy application. For example, visiting RCERO in Ljubljana showed the high-quality compost produced after composting activities, the technology used to treat mixed waste and recover useful materials (metal, plastics, etc.), and the little smell that is perceived in the area.

In some cases, waste utilities create academies, with a calendar of seminars and courses advertised through websites and brochures (Box 5.9).

For example, LIPOR makes great efforts to engage the community and all stakeholders in circular economy practices, promoting behavioral change in the entire waste management value chain, from citizens to waste utilities. In 2018, LIPOR released its 15th Sustainability Report, demonstrating a high and long-term commitment to transparency, stakeholder engagement, sustainable development, and the resulting economic, social, and environmental performance.

Box 5.9

Waste Management Academy throughout Europe – The Contarina and LIPOR Cases

Contarina Academy is the school of environmental education and training of Contarina SpA, which explores the themes of sustainable development, circular economy, and waste management according to the Contarina model. Its strong point is the active participation of all citizens along with local administrators and authorities.

Contarina Academy addresses several stakeholders for environmental education and continuous training: managers, public and private companies, local authorities, freelances, but also citizens, professionals, and the school world. The goal of this activity is the identification of shared best practices to develop an organizational culture at all levels.

The training is developed with training meetings and also educational projects for schools, teachers, and pupils to learn shared ecosustainable practices, such as waste reduction and recycling. This training activity has evolved over time in a capillary way and has attracted the interest of many Italian local administrations and even European and non-European ones who are asking for help to activate this model in their realities and to implement it with continuous training.

All training activities proposed by Contarina Academy have ISO 29990 certification, the international standard for "informal" training, i.e., lifelong learning and continuous learning. Contarina Academy offers know-how that comes from 25 years of experience in the waste field, and the objectives that it sets are the dissemination of knowledge of the Contarina model and primarily, the awareness of sustainable development and circular economy. All this is achieved using comparisons to develop the theme of waste management, as well as enhance and develop the business know-how.

LIPOR training center (Academia LIPOR) provides a set of several courses such as specialized technical training for technicians, e-learning training, accredited teacher training, practical training in organic farming, composting, and gardening. During 2018, LIPOR's Academia provided 50 training courses, i.e., 340 training hours for more than 1,000 trainees.

LIPOR Academy is certified by DGERT (General Direction of Employment and Labor Relations) and by the CEFA (Foundation for Studies and Training for Local Government). LIPOR is also accredited by Ordem dos Engenheiros (Engineering Bar). LIPOR Academy's training offer extends to different areas of knowledge.

There are many courses planned each year. For example, dozens of different courses are planned in 2020 such as regarding sustainable food and reducing biowaste, home composting and food waste, pest and disease control in the garden, environmental education, citizenship and sustainability, principles of the circular economy in waste management, green public procurement, upcycling, management of civic amenity sites, and waste management in events.

5.4 KNOWLEDGE SHARING[5]

Recently, EU Commission affirmed that *additional efforts are necessary to support the Member States in waste management. Half of them are at risk of non-compliance with the 2020 target to recycle 50% of municipal waste. To drive policy reforms, the Commission will organise high-level exchanges on the circular economy and waste and step up cooperation with Member States, regions and cities in making the best use of EU funds. Where necessary, the Commission will also use its enforcement powers* (European Commission, 2020a).

Thus, European policymakers are determining the best way to allow circulation of knowledge among countries at macrolevel, i.e., exploiting knowledge sharing among municipalities and waste operators at mesolevel,

5 The section was written by Giulia Romano.

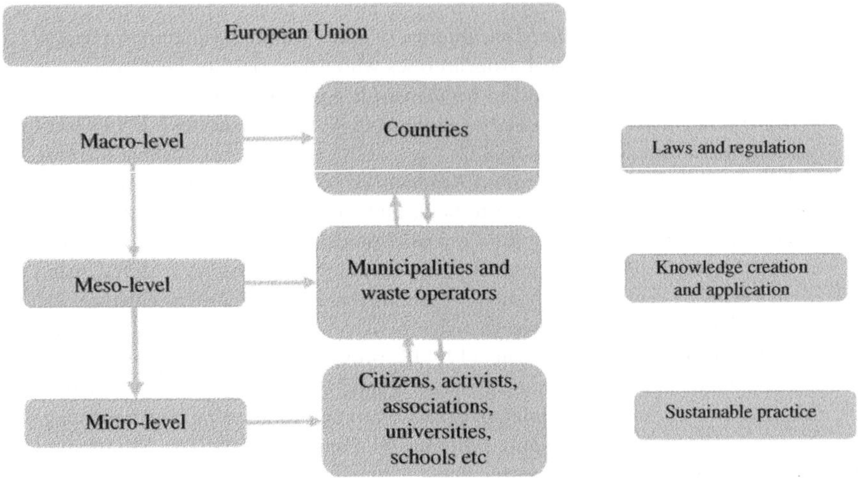

Fig. 5.3. Knowledge Sharing at Macro-, Meso-, and Microlevels.

and among citizens, activists, associations, universities, schools, and others at microlevel (Fig. 5.3).

The European normative framework can harmonize separate waste collection systems, defining *the most effective combinations of separate collection models, the density and accessibility of separate collection points, including in public spaces, taking account of regional and local conditions ranging from urban to outermost regions. Other aspects that facilitate consumer involvement will also be considered, such as common bin colours, harmonised symbols for key waste types, product labels, information campaigns and economic instruments* (European Commission, 2020).

They can also foster new knowledge creation on urban waste management throughout Europe. Indeed, *EU waste laws have driven major improvements in waste management since the 1970s, supported by EU funds. However, they need to be modernised on an ongoing basis to make them fit for the circular economy and the digital age* (European Commission, 2020). As a consequence, European countries can create the most suitable normative framework to better exploit knowledge creation at country level, driven by fiscal and public funding and leveraging progresses and innovations. Indeed, they can provide operators with economic opportunities to invest in newly developed technology, sustain reorganization processes, and extend good practices to other contexts.

EU countries exploit their knowledge in effective, sustainable, and value-creating urban waste management practices by considering relevant experiences developed at municipal and firm levels. The Milan example is currently studied and analyzed by policymakers, managers, and activists throughout Europe, highlighting the relevance of realizing and then sharing experiences, developed under public management in public utility sectors, in a public knowledge sharing network. Similarly, the Voka Snaga and LIPOR experiences are also spread through EU communication channels (European Commission, 2020c).

As previously said, innovation could be driven by accurate laws and regulation that could foster the needs at municipal and firm level in several ways to generate changes in habits and standard practices. Laws and regulation by national and local policymakers are essential to rapidly drive operators to adopt best practices, creating, for example, benchmarking and sunshine regulatory tools.

The need to produce and disseminate data for regulatory reasons allowed to use these data as relevant managerial information to drive decision-making among managers. Further, they can be easily used to produce accurate and informative sustainability reporting to reach all relevant stakeholders.

In fact, knowledge is generated at mesolevel and directly applied, through the relevant ideas and operational interchange among policymakers (frequently involved as owners of waste operators and always as local politicians and regulators), managers, employees, partners, suppliers, and through collaboration with other municipalities and waste operators (Fig. 5.3).

As already said, a good collaboration among policymakers and managers of waste operators is essential to generate new knowledge and find effective ways to put them into practice. Further, as affirmed by Agranoff (2007), *Organization – public and nonpublic – …network for public purposes, sharing information or matching services, or solving policy problems. Working in this increasingly important public network has become part of the job of public manager* (p. 2).

Lastly, generation and application of new knowledge needs direct collaboration and involvement of all relevant stakeholders from citizens, universities, and school to activists and civil society associations; to spread knowledge, data, information, and best practices among future generations of managers, citizens, activists, and policymakers.

Relevant stakeholders are also a factor affecting the knowledge sharing approach. Indeed, associations and activists have an increasingly relevant role in requiring to firms, politicians, and civil servant the creation of formal or informal relationships with other contexts, where the best practices are identified. As highlighted by Agranoff (2007), *nonchartered networks …can prove to be equally viable bodies* (p. 7).

Indeed, sustainable practices applied at microlevel also need to be shared to become benchmark to be followed and replicated, e.g., regarding home composting, ZW solutions for events organized by associations, creation, and management of reuse centers and shops, among others.

An increasingly relevant, although invisible, network interested in creating and sharing best practices and new ideas about urban waste management is growing among policymakers, managers, and practitioners throughout Europe and further. This network is made by women and men, operating in public administrations as civil servants and policymakers or as managers in waste management firms, with great expertise and increasing capacity of knowledge transfer. They are animated by innovative ideas, ready to be tested, and implemented in new contexts needing change or renovation.

The network seems to be made by experts that, at the beginning of their experience in the waste management industry, were considered mainly as visionaries, as people that proposed ideas impossible to realize, at least at a broader level than that of experimental plants or in small municipal contexts. Nowadays, these experts have developed a wider experience, and the urban waste management industry demonstrated the ability to introduce and realize relevant management and technological innovations that seemed impossible only few decades ago.

Knowledge sharing helps to exploit the best practices implemented by "waste management champions" at a broader level than that of the communities served. Then, innovations in waste management are applied in different contexts with a contingency approach to adapt practices to each context, building new knowledge on the one already existing, and shared by other municipalities, firms, and operators.

Being part of the knowledge sharing network includes sharing competences and even resources to create a broader best practice, i.e., share further examples throughout a region, a country, and even a continent where to implement innovative approaches that lead to sustainable results.

In Italy, experiences of formal collaborations between municipalities and waste firms have been realized. In Tuscany, ASCIT recently developed a first institutional collaboration with another company of the Retiambiente group, of which ASCIT has been part since 2015, REA SpA. The memorandum of understanding provides that some ASCIT employees and collaborators, including the general manager, carry out their activity for a few days at REA to streamline the transfer of knowledge and good practices developed by ASCIT to REA, facilitating the latter in the strategic and management paths undertaken, from the increase in separate waste collection to the introduction of PAYT tariff system.

Further, as previously said, Contarina realized partnerships with two startups, one in the same Veneto Region called Valpe Ambiente and the other in another Italian Region (Emilia-Romagna) called Alea Ambiente. The absence of rivalry owing to the rules of in-house provision in public service implies that successful publicly owned firms can share their business models and intellectual capital with other firms and municipalities at affordable prices.

The contribution of European policymaking could be essential to further exploit the potentialities of this network by giving resources and infrastructures to fuel this growing network of knowledge interchange.

Ad hoc solutions could be built on existing good experiences using a contingency approach, addressing emerging needs by starting the implementation of best practices, with the support of past experiences in similar contexts and avoiding past mistakes or misinterpretations of rules.

The existing experiences seem to demonstrate the ability to apply best practices in a rapid way through the lead of experts with past relevant experiences. This quick implementation leads to fulfill challenges and targets in a short period of time. The intrinsic knowledge of this already existing network is ready to be spread as much as possible in other territories outside their direct area of activity.

Knowledge sharing is common where rivalry is not an issue, i.e., when network members operate in a publicly owned context, in municipalities, local governments, or publicly owned firms where the competition is not considered as a limitation to the knowledge sharing opportunity.

For example, LIPOR in Portugal has an internationalization strategy based on the sale and provision of international consultancy services, taking advantage of the knowledge and experience that LIPOR and its team have acquired. As a result of its activity provided at the service of the community, municipalities and other stakeholders could ask the support of LIPOR for design, adoption, and implementation of sustainable waste management solutions. In 2018, LIPOR established business relationships.

The study of best practices and the exploitation and growth of this network led to discussion of an existing "alliances of good and respectable people" ("alleanze delle persone perbene") that was evoked by Water Ganapini in the early 2000s (Ganapini, 2002).

CONCLUSION: CONSIDERING THE LINKAGE BETWEEN OWNERSHIP AND CORPORATE GOVERNANCE, KEY DRIVERS OF GOOD WASTE MANAGEMENT AND PERFORMANCE UNDER THE ZERO WASTE FRAMEWORK[1]

ABSTRACT

The chapter illustrates the relationships between concepts, theories, and processes presented so far in the book.

The cases explored show how this model can be recognized first and foremost in publicly owned waste operators linked to the territory where the service is provided. The content that justifies and legitimizes their presence is that of the integral recovery of materials through the zero waste strategy.

Innovation, responsibility, stakeholder engagement, and knowledge sharing have been highlighted as the four key drivers of sustainable urban waste management. These drivers reciprocally reinforce each other in a virtuous exploitation system that generates a positive circular path of new managerial and technical resources and competencies, and new responsibility schemes shared among managers, policymakers, employees, and users.

Further, each key driver impacts the economic, environmental, and social performance of urban waste operators, increasing the overall impact and strengthening the effect of the other drivers in a virtuous exploitation of benefits for waste operators and stakeholders beyond the served territory.

Keywords: Public ownership; remunicipalization processes; knowledge sharing; performance; stakeholder engagement; waste management

1 This chapter was written by Giulia Romano and Claudio Marciano. The authors contributed equally.

Through the multiple case design, this study investigated relevant cases of urban waste operators in Italy and throughout Europe. These cases have been selected via the snowball sampling technique.

Considering similarities among cases, all the case studies share the same ownership status, i.e., they are all publicly owned waste operators that are operating as independent firms, a consortium of municipalities, and municipal bodies. They are directly owned by municipalities or indirectly through consortiums. The cases are well rooted in the idea of urban waste management as a public service aimed at granting universal access and equitable supply (Broadbent & Guthrie, 2008), wherein the main goals are better defined and pursued through a public management model. Indeed, some of these case studies are the result of remunicipalization processes, followed after inadequate results and outcomes of the privatization path.

Although the in-house provision of local public services has enjoyed a certain regulatory continuity at European level, the practice of contracts and service concessions to joint or entirely private companies has established itself as a preferred practice since the 1990s. Therefore, the privatization of public services has become one of the most relevant pillars of what critical school theorists call municipal neoliberalism (Brenner, Marcuse, & Maier, 2012; Kitchin, 2019).

The neoliberal discourse has penetrated a cultural context strongly influenced by the idea that public governance would be effective if it functioned as a facilitator rather than an entrepreneur (Harvey, 2011). The mechanisms that would have made the private market efficient in terms of profit maximization and cost reduction would have also applied to the apparatus that had remained the exclusive monopoly of the State or its local articulations. The neoliberal narrative has also asserted itself by showing the limits, such as inefficiency, corruption, low propensity for innovation, for which public management would be responsible.

The forms that this discourse has taken in waste management are numerous: private entrepreneurial actors dealing with waste treatment or disposal and others specializing in urban waste collection and hygiene services, or supplies. In several cases, waste privatization has taken hybrid forms, such as mixed companies with public and private capital, or with the stock exchange listing of public utilities, often multiple services. Another, perhaps even deeper, form through which municipal neoliberalism has taken root in waste management is through the standardization of expertise involved in managing processes and organizing services, both corporate and academic.

However, it is significant that none of these experiences are among those surveyed in our book. On the contrary, often, most private or mixed systems could be adequate to describe what we have defined in the previous chapters as the "take-make-waste" model, based on roadside collections and incineration.

In fact, we have not observed a correlation between performance in the field of cost reduction, ecological impact indicators, or civic engagement practices in subjects other than those with total public capital. This could be explained by: (1) A conflict between the return on invested capital (e.g., in the construction of an incinerator that gives high margins and long term) and the achievement of very high percentages of separate collection; (2) A private entity operating in a public service winning short-term contracts/concessions, which is incompatible with the realization of long-term investments, especially in the field of plant engineering; (3) The separation, due in the case of private individuals, in the entities in charge of managing waste treatment plants and waste collection services, which creates conflicts of interest and prevents the setting up of an efficient planning logic; (4) A public entity having a vocation and legitimacy to operate in the territory other than a private one, accepting to make investments and adopt organizational devices that are not immediately remunerative, but are useful for inducing new social behaviors or to meet environmental needs.

It is no coincidence that when zero waste (ZW) consolidated itself as a political and cultural discourse, the discourse on the common goods was also established. This positioned the idea of new processes of valorization based on sharing and social responsibility, the center of the public debate; it also implied that areas in which the market can achieve efficiency alone must be separated from those needing strong public governance in the field of implementation.

In this volume, we have proposed a model to analyze the performance of entrepreneurial actors involved in waste management, and each case seems to weigh in favor of public ownership of assets (Fig. 1).

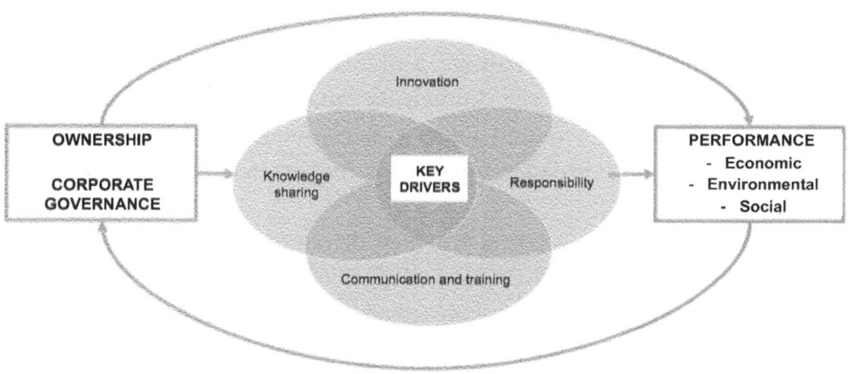

Fig. 1. Relationships among Ownership, Key Drivers, and Performance in a Triple Bottom Line (TBL) Approach.

Innovation, responsibility, stakeholder engagement, and knowledge sharing have been highlighted as the four key drivers of sustainable urban waste management. These drivers are concurrently present in all the management models of waste operators investigated. They reciprocally reinforce each other in a virtuous exploitation system that generates a positive circular path of new managerial and technical resources and competencies, and new responsibility schemes shared among managers, policymakers, employees, and also users, i.e., citizens, firms, public administration.

Innovative ideas, realized projects, and defined responsibility schemes should be communicated to stakeholders, with deep engagement of all relevant stakeholders, to inform, instill, and if necessary, even enforce new approaches and changes in habits.

Innovation without responsibility and stakeholders' engagement could be useless. In the case of a new managerial system to separately collect waste through door-to-door collection systems, if citizens are not convinced of the importance of a good separate collection at source, they will not exert adequate efforts in separation, and a large quantity of mixed waste will be produced. Additionally, if they do not believe that separately collected waste is then effectively recycled, they will devote less time in separating at source.

Similarly, responsibility and stakeholder engagement would be ineffective without proper innovation, as the commitment of stakeholders and employees is not exploited into adequate solution for sustainable waste management. For example, the absence of necessary plants or detailed and clear strategic plans can render the efforts of separate collection and citizen commitment to pursuing virtuous behavior completely ineffective.

Knowledge sharing can result in pooling of knowledge of each waste operator. Adopting a knowledge sharing approach involves being part of a formal and mostly informal network of committed managers, public servants, administrators, policymakers, and activists that concur to attract and import new knowledge from national and international relevant experiences inside the firm. Further, the knowledge sharing approach allows the sharing of knowledge acquired under other contexts and from interested stakeholders within a broader framework that stretches beyond the territories served.

Therefore, knowledge sharing is a key driver of successful urban waste management. In fact, the existing knowledge network could be the source of ideas, practices, and solutions already tested in a similar context that provides the best method to increase responsibility, exploit innovation, and create adequate and effective stakeholder engagement practices.

Case studies highlight the relevance of public ownership in generating and activating the opportunities derived from all these key drivers in a virtuous circle. Thus, although European Union (EU) rules apply equally to all kind of waste operators, ownership and corporate governance structures and rules influence strategies, policies, and results owing to their central role in decision-making processes and shaping of values and missions (Cruz & Marques, 2012; Romano & Molinos-Senante, 2020; Tavares & Camões, 2010; Voorn, Van Genugten, & van Thiel, 2017).

Public ownership allowed the design and pursuit of long-term strategies and the realization of innovation that required investment, with medium- to long-term returns. Investment is also sustained by renouncing the receiving of dividends, generating a self-financing flow that could be invested in innovation at managerial and technical levels.

Indeed, corporate governance rules are relevant in shaping best practice-compliant corporate governance systems for public waste operators, selecting most suited managers and board members, and avoiding the risks of inefficient management, corruption, and other misadministration.

Board diversity in terms of gender, professionalism, and age should also be pursued. When selecting the best managers and board members, it is of utmost importance to devote the required attention to the independence, honorability, and professionalism, expected of selected board members and managers.

Direct and in-house provisions eliminate the problem of concession expiration, which impacts strategic planning, investment realization, and value creation and distribution among stakeholders. Strategic planning outside the constraints of deadlines has a long-term orientation and reduces managerial myopia.

Responsibility directly links municipalities, waste operators, and citizens. Citizens are indirect owners of the waste operators and could affect their policies and organizational choices through elected politicians and public managers appointed in specific roles. Publicly owned waste operators must be directly accountable to the municipality (owners) and indirectly to the citizens (indirect owners). Thus, responsibility and accountability regarding quality of service, social impact, and environmental respect can be ensured.

Publicly owned waste operators are requested to be responsible, regarding not only the economic and legal aspects but also the particular ethical and philanthropic considerations required by both citizens and local authorities (Carroll, 1991).

Stakeholder engagement and socioenvironmental responsibility reporting are also linked to the ownership structure (Prado-Lorenzo, Gallego-Alvarez, &

Garcia-Sanchez, 2009), as dominant shareholders could define corporate values and organizational goals and then address their fulfillment (Thomsen & Pedersen, 2000). Public shareholders such as municipalities and other local governments have the willingness to engage stakeholder in the decision-making process embedded with their status (Romano, Rapposelli, & Marrucci, 2019; Romano & Molinos-Senante, 2020).

Public ownership also has a relevant role for the knowledge sharing approach (Minoja & Romano, 2021). In fact, where rivalry is not an issue, i.e., where public direct provision of waste services or in-house provision by publicly owned waste utilities is granted, value system and strategies can include the possibility of sharing acquired knowledge and the whole intellectual capital with other territories, firms, and public managers to generate new knowledge from preexisting and successfully applied ideas and solutions (Minoja & Romano, 2021).

Knowledge sharing is becoming part of the management model of several waste management firms, with the aim to spread ideas and practical experience regarding the best sustainable waste management practices and solutions at the service of communities, municipalities, and all interested stakeholders beyond the borders of the territory directly served.

The agreement between municipalities and firms should be based on the principle of sharing both tangible and intangible resources (know-how, human resources, technology, etc.). This exchange allows the creation of a network of companies having a streamlined organizational and operational structure along with direct contact with their territories. This enables their operation over a vast territory, not through a single large waste firm but through small to medium local firms directly controlled by the municipalities served and indirectly controlled by citizens living in the served territory. It is a management model that relies on the knowledge sharing approach and the capability of waste operators to better understand the territory, following the realization of a local public service. Indeed, stakeholder engagement and responsibility are directly exploited through public management models, wherein citizens are indirectly involved in ownership and management of waste operators, which should answer the requirements of municipalities and policymakers.

The exploitation of these four key drivers (Innovation, Responsibility, Stakeholder Engagement, and Knowledge Sharing) allowed fulfillment of challenging targets, affecting economic, environmental, and social dimensions Table 1.

Innovation has an economic impact on the performance achieved, as it increases efficiency, thus lowering costs and providing opportunities to

Table 1. Linkage between Key Drivers and Performance Results.

Key Drivers	Performance Impacts
Innovation	**Economic**: efficiency (lower costs, more services); lower costs to manage mixed waste. **Environmental**: higher recycling rate; composting. **Social**: fewer accidents at work.
Responsibility	**Economic**: higher revenues from selling recyclables and compost; lower cost for treatment of mixed waste. **Environmental**: higher recycling rate; composting; lower waste generation. **Social**: more jobs for labor-intensive business model; spreading proenvironmental behaviors.
Stakeholder Engagement	**Economic**: higher investments in consensual projects. **Environmental**: higher recycling rate; composting; lower waste generation. **Social**: higher consensus; higher stakeholder satisfaction.
Knowledge sharing	**Economic**: revenues from consulting activities. **Environmental**: higher recycling rate; composting; lower waste generation from new ideas derived from other experiences. **Social**: exploitation of knowledge in other contexts, generation of new jobs, higher quality services and customer satisfaction, and more employees.

increase service quantity and improve service quality. Further, it decreases the costs of managing mixed waste, by ensuring higher recycling rates and realizing high-quality compost to be used in agriculture. From a social perspective, innovation can improve labor conditions, increasing the safety for workers.

Responsibility leads to higher commitment of citizens toward ensuring waste reduction and separation. This should be supported by the same commitment as that of the waste operator in collecting and treating waste efficiently and effectively, realizing an efficient collection, high-quality services, recycling, and composting through the innovations exploited and applied.

This responsibility permits the realization of revenues from selling recyclables and compost. Further, it fosters cost reduction for treatment of mixed waste. From an environmental point of view, responsibility can increase the recycling rate and composting, and ensure reduction in waste generation. In addition, as responsibility is linked to appropriate separation at source and door-to-door collection methods, it creates a business model that is labor intensive, creating more jobs, and promoting proenvironmental behavior. Thus, responsibility leads to a higher involvement in meeting social targets, such as by creating a labor-intensive instead of capital-intensive business model.

Stakeholder engagement supports the implementation of consensual strategies and policies between waste operators and citizens. From an economic perspective, it requires higher investments in consensual projects that meet the expectations of waste operators and stakeholders.

Stakeholder engagement pushes toward the achievement of improved composting and recycling rates, and lower waste generation. Further, higher consensus and stakeholder satisfaction are relevant for public service provision, stressing the relevance of improving welfare conditions and prosperity among communities.

Finally, knowledge sharing allows the attainment of revenue from consulting activities and gain inspiration from other experiences to realize higher environmental targets. From a public service perspective, the exploitation of existing knowledge in other contexts allows for proper and complete realization of the public waste operator mission. Further, it helps produce new jobs, higher quality services, and higher employee and customer satisfaction.

Each key driver impacts the economic, environmental, and social performance of urban waste operators. As suggested in Table 1, each one increases the overall impact by strengthening the effect of the other drivers in a virtuous exploitation of benefits for waste operators and stakeholders beyond the served territory.

REFERENCES

Agranoff, R. (2007). *Managing within networks. Adding value to Publci Organization*. Washington, DC: Georgetown University Press.

ANAC (2019). Audizione del Presidente Raffaele Cantone, Commissione Parlamentare di Inchiesta sulle attività illecite connesse al ciclo dei rifiuti e su illeciti ambientali ad essi correlati - 30 gennaio 2019.

Arena, U., Ardolino, F., & Di Gregorio, F. (2016). Technological, environmental and social aspects of a recycling process of post-consumer absorbent hygiene products. *Journal of Cleaner Production*, *127*, 289−301.

Ball, A., & Grubnic, S. (2007). Sustainability accounting and accountability in the public sector. In J. Unerman, J. Bebbington, & B. O'Dwyer (Eds.), *Sustainability accounting and accountability* (pp. 243–265). London: Routledge.

Baratta, G. (2006). Umanesimo della convivenza: Edward Said in dialogo con Antonio Gramsci. In I. Chambers (Ed.), *Esercizi di Potere* (pp. 27–37). Roma: Meltemi.

Becker, S., Beveridge, R., & Naumann, M. (2015). Remunicipalization in German cities: Contesting neo-liberalism and reimagining urban governance? *Space and Polity*, *19*(1), 76−90.

Bel, G., & Gradus, R. (2018). Privatisation, contracting-out and inter-municipal cooperation: New developments in local public service delivery. *Local Government Studies*, *44*(1), 11−21.

Bel, G., & Warner, M. E. (2016). Factors explaining inter-municipal cooperation in service delivery: A meta-regression analysis. *Journal of Economic Policy Reform*, *19*(2), 91−115.

Benito- López, B., Moreno-Enguix, M. D. R., & Solana-Ibañez, J. (2011). Determinants of efficiency in the provision of municipal street-cleaning and refuse collection services. *Waste Management*, *31*(6), 1099–1108.

Berg, S. V., & Phillips, M. A. (2017). Data availability as a key tool for regulating government-owned water utilities. *Utilities Policy*, *49*, 30–37.

Berg, S. V. (2020). Performance assessment using key performance indicators (KPIs) for water utilities: A primer. *Water Economics and Policy*, *6*(2), 2050001.

Bergh, A., Erlingsson, G., Gustafsson, A., & Wittberg, E. (2019). Municipally owned enterprises as danger zones for corruption? How politicians having feet in two camps may undermine conditions for accountability. *Public Integrity*, *21*(3), 320–352.

BIO Intelligence Service. (2011a). Implementing EU waste legislation for green growth. Final Report prepared for European Commission DG ENV. Retrieved from https://ec.europa.eu/environment/waste/studies/pdf/study%2012%20FINAL%20REPORT.pdf

BIO Intelligence Service. (2011b). Naples: Waste management crisis. In *Implementing EU waste legislation for green growth*. Final report prepared for European commission DG ENV. Retrieved from https://ec.europa.eu/environment/waste/studies/pdf/study%2012%20FINAL%20REPORT.pdf

BiPRO/CRI. (2015). Assessment of separate collection schemes in the 28 capitals of the EU. Final report. November 2015. Retrieved from https://ec.europa.eu/environment/waste/studies/pdf/Separate%20collection_Final%20Report.pdf

Bognetti, G., & Robotti, L. (2007). The provision of local public services through mixed enterprises: The Italian case. *Annals of Public and Cooperative Economics*, *78*(3), 415–437.

Bonomi, A., Della Puppa, F., & Masiero, R. (2017). *La società circolare. Fordismo, capitalismo molecolare, sharing economy*. Milan: Derive e Approdi.

Bourdieu, P. (1992). *Il senso pratico*. Rome: Armando Editore.

Bourgeois, L. J., III, & Eisenhardt, K. M. (1988). Strategic decision process in high velocity environments: Four cases in the microcomputer industry. *Management Science*, *34*(7), 816–835.

Bratina, B., Sorgo, A., Kramberger, U., Lidija, A., Zemlijic, F., Janez, E., & Safaric, R. (2016). From municipal/industrial wastewater sludge and FOG to fertilizer: A proposal for economic sustainable sludge management. *Journal of Environmental Management*, *183*(3), 1009–1025.

Brenner, N., Marcuse, P., & Maier, M. (2012). *Cities for people, not for profit: Critical urban theory and the right to the city*. London: Routledge.

Broadbent, J., & Guthrie, J. (2008). Public sector to public services: 20 years of "contextual" accounting research. *Accounting, Auditing & Accountability Journal*, *21*(2), 129–169.

Calabrò, P. S., & Komilis, D. (2019). A standardized inspection methodology to evaluate municipal solid waste collection performance. *Journal of Environmental Management*, *246*, 184–191.

Cambridge Econometrics, Trinomics, & ICF. (2018). Impacts of circular economy policies on the labour market. Retrieved from https://op.europa.eu/en/publication-detail/-/publication/fc373862-704d-11e8-9483-01aa75ed71a1/language-en

Carroll, A. B. (1991). The pyramid of corporate social responsibilities: Toward the moral management of organizational stakeholders. *Business Horizons*, *34*(4), 39–48.

Castells, M. (1997). An introduction to the information age. *City*, *2*(7), 6–16.

Cecere, G., & Corrocher, N. (2016). Stringency of regulation and innovation in waste management: An empirical analysis on EU countries. *Industry and Innovation*, *23*(7), 625–646.

CEE Bankwatch Network. (2019). EU bank drops Belgrade incinerator, citing impact on recycling: EBRD and other banks press on - Bankwatch (online), June 24, 2020. Retrieved from https://bankwatch.org/press_release/eu-bank-drops-belgrade-incinerator-citing-impact-on-recycling-ebrd-and-other-banks-press-on

Cianciullo, A., & Fontana, E. (2005). *Dark economy. La mafia dei veleni.* Torino: Einaudi.

Clifton, J., Warner, M. E., Gradus, R., & Bel, G. (2019). Re-municipalization of public services: Trend or hype? *Journal of Economic Policy Reform*. doi: 10.1080/17487870.2019.1691344

Colaianni, G. (2008). Creatività e Innovazione individuale. *`DiPAV - Quaderni*, *21*, 29–44. Milano: Franco Angeli.

Comitato Corporate Governance (2020). *Corporate Governance Code, January 2020.* (online), June 24, 2020. Retrieved from https://www.borsaitaliana.it/comitato-corporate-governance/codice/2020eng.en.pdf

Connett, P. (2013). *The zero waste solution.* White River Junction, VT: Chelsea Green Publishing.

Contarina Spa. (2019). Bilancio di sostenibilità 2018. (online), March 12, 2020. Retrieved from https://contarina.it/files/filemanager/source/documenti/Bilancio_di_sostenibilita_2018.pdf

Conti, L. (1988). *Ambiente - Terra*. Milano: Mondadori.

Corvellec, H., Bramryd, T., & Hultman, J. (2011). The business model of solid waste management in Sweden—a case study of two municipally-owned companies. *Waste Management Research*, *30*(5), 512–518.

Cruz, N., & Marques, R. C. (2012). Mixed companies and local governance: No man can serve two masters. *Public Administration*, *90*(3), 737–758.

Curran, T., & Williams, I. D. (2012). A zero waste vision for industrial networks in Europe. *Journal of Hazardous Materials*, 207–208, 3–7. doi:10.1016/j.jhazmat.2011.07.122

D'Inverno, G., Carosi, L., & Romano, G. (2020). Environmental sustainability and service quality beyond economic and financial indicators: A performance evaluation of Italian water utilities. *Socio-Economic Planning Sciences*. (in press). doi:10.1016/j.seps.2020.100852

Dansero, E., Putilli, M., & Tacco, N. (2015). Geopolitiche dei rifiuti. Attori, scale e processi decisionali nella localizzazione di due inceneritori in Provincia di Torino. *Bollettino della società geografica italiana*, *8*, 469–490.

DANVA. (2017). Principles for good corporate governance in utilities owned by the municipalities. September. (online). April 13, 2020. Retrieved from https://www.danva.dk/media/3757/12-10-17-vejledning-good-governance-in-municipally-owned-utilities-ver6.pdf

Davis, G. G., & Hall, J. A. (2006). Circular economy legislation. The international experience. (online). December 06, 2019. Retrieved from https://view.officeapps.live.com/op/view.aspx?src=http%3A%2F%2Fsiteresources.worldbank.org%2FINTEAPREGTOPENVIRONMENT%2FResources%2FCircularEconomy_Legal_IntExperience_ExecSummary_EN.doc

De Jong, J., & Den Hartog, D. (2008). Innovative work behaviour: Measurement and validation. *Scales Research Reports H200820*, EIM Business and Policy Research.

De La Cruz, A., Medina, A., & Tang, Y. (2019). *Owners of the world's listed companies*. Paris: OECD Capital Market Series. Retrieved from www.oecd.org/corporate/Owners-of-the-Worlds-Listed-Companies.htm

Del Torre, D. (2008). Antecedenti individuali del comportamento innovative. *DiPAV - Quaderni*, *21*, 61–70. Franco Angeli.

Della Porta, D., & Diani, M. (2020). *Social movement: An introduction.* Oxford: John Wiley & Sons.

Díaz-Villavicencio, G., Didonet, S. R., & Dodd, A. (2017). Influencing factors of eco-efficient urban waste management: Evidence from Spanish municipalities. *Journal of Cleaner Production*, *164*, 1486−1496

Donaldson, L. (2001). *The contingency theory of organizations.* Thousand Oaks, CA: SAGE Publications.

Dyer, J., Gregersen, H., & Christensen, C. M. (2011). *The Innovator's Dna. Mastering the five skills of disruptive innovators.* Boston, MA: Harvard Business Review Press.

Eccles, R. G., Krzus, M. P., Rogers, J., & Serafeim, G. (2012). The need for sector-specific materiality and sustainability reporting standards. *Journal of Applied Corporate Finance*, *24*(2), 65−71.

Eisenhardt, K. M., & Graebner, M. E. (2007). Theory building from cases: Opportunities and challenges. *Academy of Management Journal*, *50*(1), 25−32.

Eisenhardt, K. M., Graebner, M. E., & Sonenshein, S. (2016). Grand challenges and inductive methods: Rigor without Rigor Mortis. *Academy of Management Journal*, *59*(4), 1113–1123. From the Editors. doi:10.5465/amj.2016.4004

Eisenhardt, K. M. (1989). Building theories from case study research. *Academy of Management Review*, *14*(4), 532−550.

Elkington, J. (1997). *Cannibals with forks. The triple bottom line of 21st century (The triple bottom line of 21st century).* Oxford: Capstone.

Elkington, J. (1998). Accounting for the triple bottom line. *Measuring Business Excellence*, *2*(3), 19−22.

Ellen MacArthur Foundation. (2015). Towards a circular economy: Business rationale for an accelerated transition. (online). Retrieved from https://www.ellenmacarthurfoundation.org/assets/downloads/TCE_Ellen-MacArthur-Foundation_9-Dec-2015.pdf?source=post_page

Ercolini, R. (2018). *Rifiuti zero. i dieci passi per la rivoluzione ecologica dal premio Nobel per l'ambiente.* Milan: Baldini+Castoldi.

EU. (2010). Being wise with waste: The EU's approach to waste management. (online). May 07, 2020. Retrieved from https://ec.europa.eu/environment/waste/pdf/WASTE%20BROCHURE.pdf

EU. (2020). *Non-financial reporting by large companies (updated rules) (europa.eu)*. Retrieved from https://ec.europa.eu/info/law/better-regulation/have-your-say/initiatives/12129-Revision-of-Non-Financial-Reporting-Directive

European Commission. (2008). Directive (EU) 2008/98 of the European Parliament and of the council. Retrieved from https://eur-lex.europa.eu/legal-content/EN/TXT/?uri=CELEX:32008L0098

European Commission. (2011). A quality framework for services of general interest in Europe. Communication from the Commission to the European Parliament, the council, the European economic and social Committee and the Committee of the regions. Brussels, December 20, 2011 COM(2011) 900 final (online). April 13, 2020. Retrieved from https://www.europarl.europa.eu/meetdocs/2009_2014/documents/com/com_com(2011)0900_/com_com(2011)0900_en.pdf

European Commission. (2013). Guide to the application of the European Union rules on state aid, public procurement and the internal market to services of general economic interest, and in particular to social services of general interest. Commission Staff Working Document. (online). October 28, 2019. Retrieved from https://ec.europa.eu/competition/state_aid/overview/new_guide_eu_rules_procurement_en.pdf

European Commission. (2014a). Report from the Commission to the Council and the European Parliament. Eu Anti-corruption report. COM (2014) 38 final, Brussels, February 3, 2014. Author. Retrieved from https://ec.europa.eu/home-affairs/sites/homeaffairs/files/e-library/documents/policies/organized-crime-and-human-trafficking/corruption/docs/acr_2014_en.pdf

European Commission. (2014b). Towards a circular economy: A zero waste programme for Europe, communication from the Commission to the European Parliament, the Council, the European economic and social committee and the committee of the regions. Brussels. July 2, 2014 COM(2014) 398 final. Author. Retrieved from https://ec.europa.eu/environment/circular-economy/pdf/circular-economy-communication.pdf

European Commission. (2015). Closing the loop — an EU action plan for the circular economy. Communication no. 614 (online). Retrieved from https://ec.europa.eu/environment/circular-economy/

European Commission. (2016). Investing in greener cities. (Online). June 13, 2020. Retrieved from https://ec.europa.eu/environment/efe/news/investing-greener-cities-2016-06-03_en

European Commission. (2018). Directive (EU) 2018/850 of the European Parliament and of the Council. Retrieved from https://eur-lex.europa.eu/legal-content/EN/TXT/PDF/?uri=CELEX:32018L0850&from=EN

European Commission. (2020a). A new circular economy action plan, for a cleaner and more competitive Europe. Communication from the Commission to the European Parliament, the Council, the European economic and social committee and the committee of the regions. COM(2020) 98 final, Brussels, March 11, 2020. Retrieved from https://ec.europa.eu/commission/presscorner/detail/en/ip_20_420

European Commission. (2020b). Services of general interest. (Online). June 24, 2020. Retrieved from https://ec.europa.eu/info/topics/single-market/services-general-interest_en

European Commission. (2020c). Ljubljana becomes the first EU capital to adopt zero waste goal. (Online). June 20, 2020. Retrieved from https://ec.europa.eu/environment/europeangreencapital/ljubljana-zero-waste-goal/

European Economic and Social Committee. (2020). Services of general interest. (Online). June 24, 2020. Retrieved from https://www.eesc.europa.eu/en/policies/policy-areas/services-general-interest

European Environmental Agency. (2015). Intensified global competition for resources (GMT 7). (online). December 06, 2019. Retrieved from https://www.eea.europa.eu/soer-2015/global/competition

European Parliament. (2020). Innovation policy. (online). June 24, 2020. Retrieved from https://www.europarl.europa.eu/factsheets/en/sheet/67/innovation-policy

Europol. (2020). Environmental crime. (online). June 20, 2020. Retrieved from https://www.europol.europa.eu/crime-areas-and-trends/crime-areas/environmental-crime

Eurostat. (2013). Glossary: Municipal waste. (Online). June 20, 2020. Retrieved from https://ec.europa.eu/eurostat/statistics-explained/index.php/Glossary:Municipal_waste

Eurostat. (2017). 477 kg of municipal waste generated per person in the EU. (online). March 01, 2018. Retrieved from https://ec.europa.eu/eurostat/web/products-eurostat-news/-/DDN-20170130-1.

Eurostat. (2019a). Waste statistics and waste management indicators. (Online). December 06, 2019. Retrieved from https://ec.europa.eu/eurostat/statistics-explained/index.php/Waste_statistics#Waste_treatmenthttps://ec.europa.eu/eurostat/statistics-explained/index.php/Waste_management_indicators#Recycling

Eurostat. (2019b). Municipal waste statistics. (Online). December 06, 2019. Retrieved from https://ec.europa.eu/eurostat/statistics-explained/index.php/Municipal_waste_statistics

Expósito, A., & Velasco, F. (2018). Municipal solid-waste recycling market and the European 2020 horizon strategy: A regional efficiency analysis in Spain. *Journal of Cleaner Production*, *172*, 938–948.

Ganapini, W. (2002). Author's reworking from "*Servizi Pubblici Locali: liberalizzazione vs privatizzazione*". Conference proceedings "Il futuro dei servizi pubblici", Archivio Osvaldo Piacentini, Reggio Emilia, June.

Ganapini, W. (2004). *Ambiente made in Italy*. Reggio Emilia: Aliberti Editore.

Gastaldi, M., Lombardi, G. V., Rapposelli, A., & Romano, G. (2020). The efficiency of waste sector in Italy: An application by DEA. Paper presented at the 2020 Connect Conference, 13–15 May, 2020, Riga. (online).

Ghisellini, P., Cialani, C., & Ulgiati, S. (2016). A review on circular economy: The expected transition to a balanced interplay of environmental and economic systems. *Journal of Cleaner Production*, *114*, 11–32.

Glaser, B., & Strauss, A. (1967). *The discovery of grounded theory. Strategies of qualitative research*. London: Wiedenfeld and Nicholson.

Golob, D. (2019). Zero waste Slovenia. (Online). May 20, 2020. Retrieved from https://slovenia.si/business-and-innovation/zero-waste-slovenia/

Guerrini, A., Carvalho, P., Romano, G., Cunha Marques, R., & Leardini, C. (2017). Assessing efficiency drivers in municipal solid waste collection services through a non-parametric method. *Journal of Cleaner Production*, *147*, 431–441.

Guthrie, J., Ball, A., & Farneti, F. (2010). Advancing sustainable management of public and not for profit organizations. *Public Management Review*, *12*(4), 449–459.

Hall, D., & Nguyen, T. A. (2012). Waste management in europe: Companies, structure and employment. PSIRU report commissioned by the European Federation of Public Service Unions (EPSU). (online). April 29, 2018.

Retrieved from http://www.psiru.org/reports/waste-management-europecompanies-structure-and-employment.html

Hall, S. (1981). Notes on deconstructing the popular. In R. Samuel (Ed.), *People's history and socialist theory*. London: Routledge.

Hall, D. (2001). *Water privatisation and quality of service*. London: Public Services International Research Unit, University of Greenwich.

Hall, D. (2012). Re-municipalising municipal services in Europe. PSIRU report commissioned by the European Federation of public service Unions (EPSU). May (revised November). (online). April 29, 2018. Retrieved from http://www.psiru.org/sites/default/files/2012-11-Remun.docx

Harvey, D. (2011). *Le città ribelli. I movimenti urbani dalla Comune di Parigi a Occupy Wall Street*. Milan: Il Saggiatore.

Homsy, G. C. (2016). Powering sustainability: Municipal utilities and local government policymaking. *Environment and Planning C: Government and Policy*, *34*(6), 1076–1094.

Iaboni, V., & De Stefanis, P. (2007). *Aspetti economici del recupero energetico*. Roma: Enea.

Kitchin, R. (2019). The timescape of smart cities. *Annals of the Association of American Geographers*, *109*(3), 775. doi:10.1080/24694452.2018.1497475

Kishimoto, S., Lobina, E., & Petitjean, O. (2015). *Our public water future: The global experience with remunicipalisation*. Amsterdam, London, Paris, Cape Town and Brussels: Transnational Institute (TNI), Public Services International Research Unit (PSIRU), Multinationals Observatory, Municipal Services Project (MSP) and the European Federation of Public Service Unions (EPSU).

Krausmann, F., Gingrich, S., Eisenmenger, N., Erb, K., Haberl, H., & Kowalski, M. F. (2009). Growth in global materials use, GDP and population during the 20th century. *Journal of Ecological Economics*, *68*, 2696–2705.

Lacy, P., & Rutqvist, J. (2015). *Waste to wealth. The circular economy advantage*. London: Palgrave Macmillan.

Laffont, J., & Tirole, J. (1991). Privatization and incentives. *Journal of Law, Economics, and Organization*, *7*(Special Issue), 84–105.

Landriani, L., Lepore, L., D'Amore, G., Pozzoli, F., & Alvino, F. (2019). Decorporatization of a municipal water utility: A case study from Italy. *Utilities Policy*, *57*, 43–47.

Lears, T. J. J. (1985). The concept of cultural hegemony: Problems and possibilities. *The American Historical Review*, *90*(3), 567–593.

Leo, S., & Salvia, M. (2017). Local strategies and action plan towards resource efficiency in South East Europe. *Renewable Sustainable Energy Review*, *68*, 286–305.

López-Gamero, M. D., Zaragoza-Sáez, P., Claver-Cortés, E., & Molina-Azorín, J. F. (2011). Sustainable development and intangibles: Building sustainable intellectual capital. *Business Strategy and the Environment*, *20*(1), 18–37. doi:10.1002/bse.666

Marciano, C., & Montani, A. R. (2012). I movimenti ambientalisti tra passato e futuro. In M. Gavrila (Ed.), *L'onda anomala dei media. Il rischio ambientale tra realtà e rappresentazione*. Milan: Franco Angeli.

Marciano, C. (2017). Economia circolare. Critica di un paradigma emergente nella policy ambientale dell'UE. *Prisma Economia-Società-Lavoro*, *1–2*, 14–25.

Marques, R. C., Simões, P., & Pinto, F. S. (2018). Tariff regulation in the waste sector: An unavoidable future. *Waste Management*, *78*, 292–300.

Massarutto, A. (2011). Anche la green economy ha una parte marrone. La gestione dei rifiuti e l'utopia "rifiuti zero". *L'Industria*, *2*, 245–264.

Mazzarella, F., Escobar-Tello, C., & Mitchell, V. (2016). Moving textile artisans' communities towards a sustainable future: A theoretical framework. In *Proceedings of 50th Anniversary Design Research Society Conference, Brighton, Great Britain*, 27–30, June 2016.

McDonald, D. A. (2018). Building a pro-public movement in Canada. *Studies in Political Economy*, *99*(1), 59–78.

McKinsey & Company. (2015). Growth within: A circular economy vision for a competitive Europe, report. (online). January 8, 2018. Retrieved from https://www.mckinsey.com/business-functions/sustainability-and-resource-productivity/our-insights/europes-circular-economy-opportunity

Menozzi, A., Gutierrez Urtiaga, M., & Vannoni, D. (2011). Board composition, political connections, and performance in state-owned enterprises. *Industrial and Corporate Change*, *21*(3), 671–698.

Minoja, M., & Romano, G. (2021). Managing intellectual capital for sustainability: Evidence from a re-municipalized, publicly owned waste management firm. *Journal of Cleaner Production*, *279*, 123213.

Nebbia, G. (1990). *La società dei rifiuti*. Bari: Edipuglia.

Nonaka, I. (1991). The knowledge creating company. *Harvard Business Review*, *69*, 96–104.

OECD. (2013). *Boards of directors of state-owned enterprises: An overview of national practices*. Paris: OECD Publishing.

OECD. (2015). *OECD guidelines on corporate governance of state-owned enterprises*. 2015 Edition. Paris: OECD Publishing. doi:10.1787/9789264244160-en

OECD. (2020). *Implementing the OECD guidelines on corporate governance of state-owned enterprises: Review of recent developments*. Paris: OECD Publishing. doi:10.1787/4caa0c3b-en

Official Statistics of Finland. (2018). Waste statistics. (online). April 20, 2020. Retrieved from http://www.stat.fi/til/jate/2018/jate_2018_2020-01-15_tie_001_en.html

Osborne, S. P., Radnor, Z., Vidal, I., & Kinder, T. (2014). A sustainable business model for public service organizations? *Public Management Review*, *16*(2), 165–172.

Ostrom, E. (1990). *Governing the commons: The evolution of institutions for collective action*. Cambridge: Cambridge University Press.

Pagni, L. (2002). Un impianto di riciclaggio sulle ceneri della Maserati. *Repubblica*, September 19.

Petersen, O. H., Hjelmar, U., & Vrangbæk, K. (2018). Is contracting out of public services still the great panacea? A systematic review of studies on economic and quality effects from 2000 to 2014. *Social Policy & Administration*, *52*, 130–157.

Pietzsch, N., Duarte Ribeiro, J. L., & de Medeiros, J. G. (2017). Benefits, challenges and critical factors of success for zero waste: A systematic literature review. *Waste Management*, *67*, 324–353.

Prado-Lorenzo, J., Gallego-Alvarez, I., & Garcia-Sanchez, I. M. (2009). Stakeholder engagement and corporate social responsibility reporting: The ownership structure effect. *Corporate Social Responsibility and Environmental Management*, *16*, 94–107.

Rigamonti, L., Sterpi, I., & Grosso, M. (2016). Integrated municipal waste management systems: An indicator to assess their environmental and economic sustainability. *Ecological Indicators*, *60*, 1–7.

Rogers, E. M. (2003). *Diffusion of innovations*. New York: The Free Press.

Romano, G., & Guerrini, A. (2014). The effects of ownership, board size and board composition on the performance of Italian water utilities. *Utilities Policy*, *31*, 18–28.

Romano, G., & Guerrini, A. (2019). Paying returns to shareholders of water utilities: Evidence from Italy. *Sustainability*, *11*(7), 2033, doi:10.3390/su11072033

Romano, G., Masserini, L., & Lombardi, G. V. (2021). Environmental performance of waste management: Impacts of corruption and public maladministration in Italy. *Journal of Cleaner Production*, *288*, 125521. doi:10.1016/j.jclepro.2020.125521

Romano, G., & Molinos-Senante, M. (2020). Factors affecting eco-efficiency of municipal waste services in Tuscan municipalities: An empirical investigation of different management models. *Waste Management*, *105*, 384–394.

Romano, G., Salvati, N., & Guerrini, A. (2018). Governance, strategy and efficiency of water utilities: The Italian case. *Water Policy*, *20*, 109–126.

Romano, G., Rapposelli, A., & Marrucci, L. (2019). Improving waste production and recycling through zero-waste strategy and privatization: An empirical investigation. *Resources, Conservation and Recycling*, *146*, 256–263.

Romano, G., Ferreira, D. C., Marques, R. C., & Carosi, L. (2020). Waste services' performance assessment: The case of Tuscany, Italy. *Waste Management*, *118*, 573–584.

Said, E. (1978). *Orientalism*. New York, NY: Pantheon Books.

Sarra, A., Mazzocchitti, M., & Rapposelli, A. (2017). Evaluating joint environmental and cost performance in municipal waste management systems through data envelopment analysis: Scale effects and policy implications. *Ecological Indicators*, *73*, 756–771.

Schleifer, A., & Vishny, R. W. (1994). Politicians and firms. *The Quarterly Journal of Economics*, *109*(4), 995–1025.

Senato Della Repubblica. (2016). Servizio studi dossier europei n. 16 and camera dei deputati, ufficio rapporti con l'unione europea n. 40 (2016). Documentazione per le Commissioni, esame di atti e documenti dell'UE. Le proposte sull'economia circolare COM(2015)614, COM(2015)595, COM(2015)596, COM(2015)593, COM(2015)594. Updated edition.

Simões, P., & Marques, R. C. (2012). On the economic performance of the waste sector: A literature review. *Journal of Environmental Management*, *106*, 40–47.

Soukopová, J., & Vaceková, G. (2018). Internal factors of intermunicipal cooperation: What matters most and why? *Local Government Studies 44* (1), 105–126.

Srivastava, P. K., Kulshreshtha, K., Mohanty, C. S., Pushpangadan, P., & Singh, A. (2005). Stakeholder-based SWOT analysis for successful municipal solid waste management in Lucknow, India. *Waste Management*, *25*(5), 531–537.

Sun, L., Yung, E. H. K., Chan, E. H. W., & Zhu, D. (2016). Issues of NIMBY conflict management from the perspective of stakeholders: A case study in Shanghai. *Habitat International*, *53*, 133–141.

Tavares, A. F., & Camões, P. J. (2010). New forms of local governance: A theoretical and empirical analysis of municipal corporations in Portugal. *Public Management Review*, *12*(5), 587–608.

Tavares, A. F. (2017). Ten years after: Revisiting the determinants of the adoption of municipal corporations for local service delivery. *Local Government Studies*, *43*(5), 697–706.

Thomsen, S., & Pedersen, T. (2000). Ownership structure and economic performance in the largest European companies. *Strategic Management Journal*, *21*, 689–705.

Tornavacca, A., & Onida, M. (1999). *Da rifiuti a risorse*. Mestre: Ecoistituto del Veneto.

Touraine, A. (1978). *La produzione della società*. Bologna: Il Mulino.

United Nations (UN). (2015). Resolution adopted by the general Assembly on 25 September 2015. (online), November 16, 2017. Retrieved from www.un.org/ga/search/view_doc.asp?symbol=A/RES/70/1&Lang=E.

United Nations Industrial Development Organization - UNIDO. (2017). Circular economy. (online). November 16, 2017. Retrieved from http://www.unido.org/what-we-do/cross-cutting-services/circular-economy.html

Vacca, G., & Rossi, A. (2007). *Gramsci tra Mussolini e Stalin*. Roma: Fazi.

Valdovinos, J. (2012). The remunicipalization of Parisian water services: New challenges for local authorities and policy implications. *Water International*, *37*(2), 107–120.

Van de Ven, A. (1999). *The innovation journey.* New York: Oxford University Press.

Vantaan Energia. (2020). Vantaa energy. (online). June 17, 2020. Retrieved from https://www.vantaanenergia.fi/en/we/vantaaenergy/

Voka Snaga (2018). Snagazin, A Magazin for a better lifestyle. Ljubljana.

Voorn, B., Van Genugten, L. M., & van Thiel, S. (2017). The efficiency and effectiveness of municipally owned corporations: A systematic review. *Local Government Studies, 43*(5), 820–841.

West, M. A., & Farr, J. L. (1990). Innovation at work. In M. A. West, & J. L. Farr (Eds.), *Innovation and creativity at work: Psychological and organizational strategies.* Chichester: Wiley.

World Bank. (2012). What a waste. A global review of solid waste management. March, No. 15. (online). November 16, 2017. Retrieved from http://documents.worldbank.org/curated/en/302341468126264791/pdf/68135-REVISED-What-a-Waste-2012-Final-updated.pdf

World Bank. (2017). Atlas of sustainable development goals 2017: From world development indicators. . (online). November 16, 2017. Retrieved from https://openknowledge.worldbank.org/handle/10986/26306

World Bank. (2020). Responsible consumption and production. (online). June 24, 2020. Retrieved from http://datatopics.worldbank.org/sdgatlas/archive/2017/SDG-12-responsible-consumption-andproduction.html

Yin, R. K. (1984). Beyond method: Strategies for social research. *Administrative Science Quarterly, 29*(2), 321–323.

Zaman, A., & Ashan, T. (2019). *Reconsidering waste management for the future.* London: Routledge.

Zaman, A. U., & Lehmann, S. (2011). Urban growth and waste management optimization towards 'zero waste city'. *City, Culture and Society*, 2, 177–187.

Zapata, P., & Zapata Campos, M. J. (2019). Cities, institutional entrepreneurship and the emergence of new environmental policies: The organizing of waste prevention in the City of Gothenburg, Sweden. *Environment and Planning C: Politics and Space, 37*(2), 339–359.

INDEX

Printed and bound by CPI Group (UK) Ltd, Croydon, CR0 4YY

13/09/2026

14961061-0007